Star Guest

A life on stage

Star Guest

A life on stage

Rob Guest

Hodder Moa Beckett

National Library of New Zealand Cataloguing-in-Publication Data
Guest, Rob, 1950-
Star Guest : a life on stage / Rob Guest.
ISBN 1-86958-814-2
1. Guest, Rob, 1950- 2. Singers—New Zealand—Biography.
3. Musicals—Australia. 4. Musicals—New Zealnd. I. Title.
792.6092—dc 21

Front cover:
Left: Publicity shot for *The Phantom*. Reproduced with permission of *Destination* magazine.
Top right: The Phantom — publicity flyer, Melbourne Premiere, Princess Theatre, December 1997
Bottom right: As Jean Valjean, from *Les Miserables* Programme — 10th Anniversary Production, Auckland Premiere, 1999.   Producer —
John Robertson; photography — Michael Le Poer Trench and Robert McFarlane. Courtesy of Cameron Mackintosh.

ISBN 1-86958-814-2

© 2002 — Design and format Hodder Moa Beckett Publishers Limited
Published in 2002 by Hodder Moa Beckett Publishers Limited
[a member of the Hodder Headline Group]
4 Whetu Place, Mairangi Bay, Auckland

Designed and produced by Hodder Moa Beckett Publishers Limited
Scanning by Microdot, Auckland
Printed by PrintLink, Wellington

Dedication

I would like to dedicate this book to my Mum and Dad
— for all their support and undying encouragement;
for the guidance they gave me while at the same time
allowing me to make my own choices; and for all the
understanding and band-aids during those early
fragile years, not to mention the handkerchiefs
and late night talks as I learned how to fly.

And I would also like to dedicate it to my wonderful
children Amy and Christopher, who, everyday, enable
me to see the world as my parents did.

Contents

Preface

FOR YEARS AND YEARS the gag's always been, 'Be very careful what you do or say because when I write my book . . . ' Well folks, here it is!

For all of you who are about to read this book with a little trepidation, allow me to put your minds at ease. This is, hopefully, a series of recollections which 'eggs the face' of only Yours Truly!

It is a journey which has taken me to places both exotic and humdrum and offered me experiences from the almost inexplicable (including a tussle with a tiger) to 'My God, I hope I never have to do this again!' It provides an insight, I hope, into the extraordinary world of a performer, from this performer's point of view. I hope you enjoy it.

Writing this book is a weird experience. It makes me take the time to look back at my life and recall the details — the funny, sad and 'would rather forget' moments that I suppose make up everyone's memories. Most of the time my retrospective makes me smile.

Much of it reminds me of what a little rogue I was and that I've done almost every wild thing my wonderful children may ever contemplate before it enters their little heads. (Be assured kids, my mother, who knows and loves you as I do, tells me I have met my match in you.) I have also been able to relive the shows that I am privileged to have been a part of over the years — let me take you on a backstage tour of a few of these later in my story. I have to say that I truly believe a performance lingers in a theatre long after you can no longer smell the greasepaint and that, on some level, the memory of a show remains for ever, hence the magical feeling we get when we visit the theatre.

I have always taken the time to spend a few moments alone in a theatre at the beginning of a season and again at the end, just to absorb the atmosphere and allow my soul to wander through the characters and moments that have built that theatre's 'personality'. Perhaps I'm a little superstitious, but I love these times, this ritual. Maybe it's just my way of appreciating my fantastic workspace.

I hope that in reading this you get a hint of the fun my life has been so far. I say 'so far' because when I was approached to write this account, it crossed my mind that a biography is so often written at the end of a career. This made me a little edgy at first, but remembering the television show 'This Is Your Life' I realised that writing about the special moments and curve balls that life has already thrown me is not saying it's all over (heaven forbid!), but 'This is me, at least so far'.

1.
Growing Up Around the World

MY LIFE BEGAN AT an early age in a hospital known as Love Day Street in Birmingham, England, but I spent my first years in the small Midlands town of Dudley, not far from Wolverhampton. My parents, Betty and John, my brother Dave and I were a very close family — ours was a warm home, filled with laughter and plenty of noise. We lived in a modest two-storey home, which was exactly the same as every other home on the estate, except for two important points. First, we were on the corner, which was great for keeping an eye on all the neighbourhood kids, and second we had an ugly great disused air-raid shelter in one fabulously overgrown section — cool! This concrete monstrosity was a wonderful source of fun and drama. Flat roofed, it was a man-made temptation for a young Pommie lad with good-natured adventure on his mind. Like most boys, trouble was a constant companion for Dave and me from the time we could walk.

We must not have been more than seven and five when we were finally able to scramble up the vine-clad walls of the bunker. The outside was always more interesting than the inside, possibly because the inside was just so creepy. It took us no time at all to begin our experiments in human flight — after watching the birds it seemed easy enough. Boy, that bunker looked a lot bigger once I was lying flat on my back staring skywards, crying and wondering what had gone wrong.

My next challenge to gravity probably aged my poor mother by 10 years. There she was, chatting with a neighbour, when a deafening scream shattered the peaceful afternoon. Both women turned to the source of the sound, to see dear lovable Rob hanging from the small window of a second-storey bedroom. My mother covered the distance between the back yard and the front door, bolted up the stairs, along

ROB GUEST COLLECTION

Robert John Guest — six months old.

the passage and into the bedroom before the echo of that scream had died. She grabbed my legs and dragged me inside just as I had begun to topple out the window. I do believe that at that moment my perplexed mother could not decide whether to paddle my rear end from then till Christmas for shortening her time on this planet, or hug the breath from me because her baby boy was safe again. I think she'd have chosen differently had she known then that the scream was one of frustration because I had become STUCK in the window-frame and it was preventing my flight. She had reached me just as I'd wriggled free — the ground was to have been my next stop. I wonder how big our house would have looked from my position on the lawn staring at the sky, crying. Thanks, Mum.

Those early years were fraught with almost daily courtship with disaster. Once, while helping Mum polish the banister I sailed face-first down a flight of stairs, hitting my nose on every step. This resulted in a frantic dash to hospital and took 27 or so years to properly heal. I never did see the nice birdie the doctor wanted me to watch as he stitched, but those spinning stars sure were bright. On yet another occasion I took advantage of my mother's absence from the room to tackle an annoying fly. No one had told me how to deal with flies, but I thought I had it. I waited for it to land, by chance upon the naked light bulb hanging from the ceiling, took a firm hold of my well-used wooden hammer, climbed a teetering stack of furniture, and with one huge blow attempted to end its life. The bulb exploded of course, showering the room with tiny shards of glass. I think my mother must have broken another world sprint record to reach me. There I was, perched precariously on a chair, upon a table, with my bright yellow hammer still in my little hand, once again crying my eyes out. Not because I had smashed the bulb and scared the living daylights out of myself, but because I had missed the fly, which was now sitting on the television screen laughing at me. If only Mum hadn't run so fast I might have had another crack at it. Remembering my childhood adventures it's a wonder I ever let my own kids out of my sight. Knowing they have inherited my Evil Knievel zest for life I have contemplated buying shares in a cotton wool factory.

Dudley is known for its zoo, which surrounds a castle once owned by Oliver Cromwell. I remember numerous family outings to see the wonderful collection of lions, tigers, elephants and so on, although I never did like the reptile house, which provides another story. Our house was close to the back fence of the zoo, so of course Mum and Dad warned us every chance they got about the dangers of trespassing on the zoo grounds and told terrifying tales of people who had gone missing in the lime pits around the castle. My brother was a little young, but my friends and I used to climb under the fence and play for hours in the zoo grounds, barely feet from the lions and lime pits. If Mum only knew . . . well I guess she does now. Sorry, Mum, I hope this hasn't cost you another 10 years!

The hills behind our home were undeveloped housing land and I often wonder what they look like now. Back then those hills rolled on into tomorrow, seemed tall as mountains and, being fairly clear of overgrowth, made a fantastic playground for games, especially cowboys and Indians. One bright day, when I was about seven and Dave around five, we were called home for lunch as usual. I was hungrily devouring a tableful of food Mum had laid out when the tranquillity was shattered by the sound of fire engines. The ringing of the bells grew louder and louder and the air became misty with smoke as the grey clouds from a fire billowed from our hills. I continued with my lunch as Mum,

Opposite page: Mum, Dave and me — Dad took the photo.

Left: My Dad — the
best in the world.

ROB GUEST COLLECTION

Right: Me and Dave
having a quiet cuppa
— actually Lucozade.

ROB GUEST COLLECTION

barely holding back panic, squealed in a whisper, 'Where's Dave?'

'I left him on the hill,' I said. 'You see, today was his turn to be the Indian.' I had tied him to a tree and tried to set fire to the bush next to him with some matches I'd pinched from home. The silly things hadn't worked properly so I'd tossed them all into the bush and trotted home leaving Dave gagged and tied to the tree. Obviously there was life in those matches after all . . . cool! Dave was OK and not a lock of his lovely blond hair was singed. My rear end should have been smoking but actually I think my kind-hearted mother just lectured my ear off instead. I'm not sure how it came about but we were given a tour of one of the bright red fire engines and I even got to ring the bell. Hardly going to put me off, is it?

We had a few pets in our time, some sadly less hardy than others, but one particularly strong and extremely patient friend was Dad's beloved boxer, 'Butch'. He won many a prize and Dad took great pride in him, grooming and fussing over him constantly. To us though, he was a great big softie and playmate who slobbered so generously we often joked about using this foaming 'shampoo' to wash the house down. One morning, having grown bored with carving fabulous rifts through the deep snow in our yard on my sled, I headed off in search of Dad's toolbox, just to see what I could find. Well, well, well . . . a big bright can of yellow lead-based paint and a huge four-inch paintbrush. After about half an hour's struggle, and two broken screwdrivers, I managed to prise the top off the can without spilling too much on the pristine concrete floor my hardworking father had poured just a few weeks earlier.

'Now, what can I paint?' I asked myself. Dad had already painted the front door, the walls were OK, I kind of liked the furniture the way it was, so . . . MY SLED! I was doing really well, not too much paint on the garage floor, only a little on my clothes and the sled was looking wonderful, when Butch appeared from nowhere. Of course, dogs being magnetically attracted to paint, he brushed all the way down the side of the very wet sled. Did I say my Dad used to groom him all the time? And I guess I did mention he was a prized, pedigree boxer, didn't I? It's funny how the young mind works — that streak of yellow paint on Butch's coat seemed to yell at me 'BOY — YOU'RE IN FOR IT NOW!' The more I looked at it the more I knew I had to destroy the evidence at all costs. Racing back to Dad's tools I found an oily rag and began a frantic attack on the rogue smear, spreading it further and further over poor Butch. Oh no! Oh no! What was I to do? I figured the family was bound to notice. What could I do? Then it occurred to me that the streaky smudge stood out because it was a different colour to the rest of Butch's coat, so I should complete the job and no one would notice! Poor Butch, he sat so still while, with that four-inch brush firmly in my hand, I created a great yellow dog. I had nearly finished, I had just his ears left to paint when Dad came around the corner . . . his timing could not have been worse. If he had just been a couple of minutes later, I'd have been finished, the paint would have been put away . . . oh well.

It took a while but Butch did get his own back. While they say that elephants have long memories, I reckon boxers have even longer ones. It was almost a month after the paint episode, and Dad and I were exercising Butch in the quarry behind the estate. We were playing fetch the ball and sometimes Butch would even run after it! Dad would throw the ball, I would take off after it, then Dad would tell Butch to go get it. I reckon that dog must have been part locomotive — he used to take a quick look at where he had to go, lower that great big head and charge like a bull in Madrid after that ball. On this occasion I found myself between Butch and his ball. From my perspective there was a huge, slobbering, mad dog coming to flatten me. He didn't even seem to be

Sunday family picnic. From left: Mum, Dave (loved getting his photo taken) Nan, me, Grandad.

ROB GUEST COLLECTION

watching, just charging straight at me. I think I can still hear the conflict of voices — Dad yelling, 'Don't move, stand still,' and the much louder voice in the back of my mind pleading with me to 'get the heck out of there — you're going to die!' Now, I knew Butch had a knack of swerving at the last second and missing anyone in his way, but I could not, absolutely could not, just stand there. I had to dodge, and Butch dodged too. Well, his solid (still slightly yellow) head walloped my thigh with a tremendous crunch, and I took my first flight (finally) at that tender age. He just shook his head wondering what had hit him and I cried buckets as Dad ran over to make sure I was still alive. Butch licked me all over, apparently satisfied with his paint job pay-back.

My life and time in England was pretty simple compared to the rat race of today, but then I guess most youngsters will see things in the same way when they grow up. The only thing they have to worry about is . . . come to think of it, what do they have to worry about? We never worried about anything as kids: school five days a week, movies on Saturday mornings, family outings on Sunday and two weeks a year at the seaside. Throw in Easter holidays and birthday celebrations and you basically have life as it was for us.

We used to walk miles and miles to school and back each day, though Mum reckons it was no more than about a kilometre. Nevertheless, it seemed to take at least an hour and a half to get home. Hmmm, that might have had something to do with the big kid at the end of our street waiting every afternoon to sit on me in the snow. It might also have taken us longer than we thought to build our snowmen and slides in the ice on each corner of the block, watching for (and rating) the slipovers of unwary passers-by. Perhaps it was just because we were physically and mentally exhausted from studying hard all day . . . with no strength left we'd just drag our feet on that long trek home. . . . Yeah right, it was the fat kid.

As Arthur Kipps in *Half A Sixpence*, 1970s. Note the platform shoes and bell bottoms.

Publicity shot for the Palmerston North production of *Sixpence,*1970s.

Poster for *Joseph and the Amazing Technicolor Dreamcoat*, **Hamilton**.

My dear friend Robert Young as Pharaoh, and me as Joseph.

Top: *Joseph* — Palmerston North rehearsal.
Left: Finale — *Joseph*.
Above: Iris Copland and myself, Balclutha. I stayed with
Iris during the Balclutha season of *Joseph*, in 1987.
We still keep in touch.

Publicity shot 1980 prior to my overseas trip to United Kingdom and the United States.

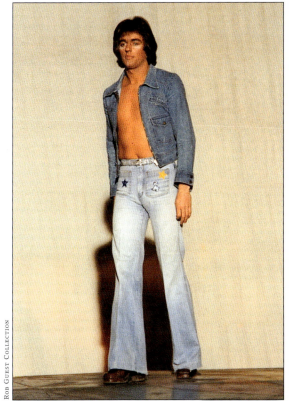

Top: 'Close Every Door', *Joseph*.
Left: Prologue rehearsal, *Joseph*.
Above: Backstage hugs after the show.
Invercargill, 1975.

Right: Accepting Professional Performer of the Year trophy from special guest presenter, the then Prime Minister, Sir Robert Muldoon, 1973.

Below: The night I was named Entertainer of the Year, at Trillos, Auckland, 1978.

I went to Sledmere school until I reached the age of 11, then to Blue Coat Secondary Modern. My years at Sledmere were mostly uneventful except that they opened my eyes to the fascination of girls, and gave me the chance to realise where I feel truly at home — on the stage. When the teachers at Sledmere called for volunteers for the 'Wild West' production my hand shot up immediately. Since I was to dress like a cowboy and sing 'She'll Be Coming Round the Mountain' I figured I could dust off the Buntline Specials from our games of Custer's Last Stand and coax Mum out of a few more rounds of caps. I remember a very out-of-tune piano and an equally tuneless pianist. I remember striding confidently out on stage wearing my red bandana, chequered cowboy shirt and short pants. It was wild! The audience was mine; I sang, they cheered, I fired my guns, they cheered, I sang, they clapped, I fixed my cap guns, they laughed. I ran out of words and started again — after all I still had caps in my guns. They could not get me off that stage, I sang the same verse until I finally ran out of caps. I was hooked from that moment. Here's my tip for all budding performers: always make sure you know the second verse, and try never to run out of caps.

By the time I changed schools I felt like an old pro. I joined the drama group and the first production I had a shot at was a play titled *Elegant Edward*, in which I played a dandy burglar who made a habit of breaking into houses dressed in a tuxedo. I can still recall being made up with greasepaint for the first time and wearing a ridiculously oversized moustache. Everybody said I looked like some chap called Douglas Fairbanks Jnr, which sounded good to me although I had no idea who he was at the time of course. This character of mine was caught by the lady of the house (played by the headmaster's daughter) who fell in love with him and let him go. For the trip home I found myself a seat at the top of the stairs on the local double-decker bus, as I felt befitted my new status. People recognised me and pointed in my direction — I had made it, I was famous! Or was it that oversized moustache and all the greasepaint I had refused to take off? I guess it looked a little out of place on an 11-year-old kid on a bus at night.

I went on to sing in the school choir where I was forever being told to 'sing quieter' (nothing changes). I reckon that my time at Blue Coat Secondary helped showbiz to find me, heaven knows none of the teachers could! For example, I never did see eye to eye with the woodwork teacher, Mr Sweeney. He finally gave me the option to 'pull my socks up or take up cooking with the girls next door'. I heard the gauntlet hit the floor, called for an apron and agreed to the cooking in my most polite manner.

The next week I lined up outside the classroom with the girls, giving the boys a field day. Comments flew back and forth between the lines of kids while I stood quietly in the middle and watched the teachers' bemused faces as they tried to work me out. Thrilled not to be dealing with woodwork and Mr Sweeney I listened as things just seemed to get better and better. There I was in a room full of giggling girls, preparing to bake my favourite dish, apple pie. It was only when the teacher started on the technicalities that I began to wonder what I had let myself in for. 'Gather and measure your ingredients,' she said. At least I knew what I was doing in woodwork — you took a piece of wood, did a bit of slashing and thrashing and voilà! A pipe rack!

The girls chipped in with the ingredients, helped me with the pastry and apples, and before long I had the biggest pie in the class plus 30 'best mates' at playtime. The next week all the boys tried to line up for cooking until Mr Sweeney arrived and I was forced after all to endure the cooking classes as the only boy — what a trial! The girls were a great help as I made jam, scones, cakes and all sorts of yummy stuff. No jibes from the boys either, just 'What's on the menu?' and lots of company at break.

H

Right: Dave and me on our yearly two-week holiday at the seaside.

Opposite page: Dad and me at Rhyl holiday camp, England. How proud am I?

For a while at this time we lived upstairs in a big old pub that Mum and Dad leased in Dudley, the Sir Robert Peel. It was a typically English local on the road to Wolverhampton, with a main public bar, a smoke room or lounge, where the best furniture and piano were kept, and a special 'out of bounds to Dave and Rob' room. Apart from the typical darts matches, the pub had its own pigeon-racing team and this special room housed the pigeon timing clocks. As with all these old pubs, the toilets were outside — and I mean couldn't be more outside, freeze your fundamentals outside, wave hello to the public outside. One particularly cold and snowy weekend morning Dave and I tired of soccer in the car park, built ourselves a snowman and lobbed snowballs at each other and anything that couldn't get away. We began pitching our snowballs onto the main roof of the pub hoping to shift a great chunk of fresh snow, but our snowballs just sank into the soft new snow with an unsatisfying thud. Just then a truck arrived with a large order of groceries and we swung open the huge wooden gates and accepted the delivery for the pub. For a while no one but us knew it was there.

Now I don't know why these things happen, what puts these ideas into our heads, but potatoes suddenly seemed like a much better piece of ammo than a snowball. If we chose our potatoes well and got the angle just right, we could cause an avalanche. I grabbed one large spud, took careful aim, pulled back and let it rip. What a shot! The slope was perfect, the boulder of snow followed by my potato rumbled down the roof towards me looming larger and larger until SPLAT. You may recall I mentioned the toilets were outside, well . . . the urinal was just beyond the eaves out back, now heavy with fresh snow. This was going to be great — Dave took a shot. A nice try for a young fella but a 'no go'. We decided to wait. It was getting late in the afternoon and the locals had been drinking for quite a while — with the beer, black pudding, cheese and crackers working their magic we would soon have a victim.

I figured when I heard the back door open, I should count to 10, throw my potato into the drift of snow on the roof beyond the urinal and if the slope was right, with a bit of luck . . . I heard the door. My heart was doing back-flips; I chose my potato, counted to 10, pulled back and fired. A huge throw — straight through the window of the spare bedroom with a startling crash. The poor bloke in the urinal had the fright of his life, since he couldn't see the window from where he was, and so ran drunkenly screaming up the road. I ducked behind a car for just long enough to realise Dave was smirking at me. I knew I was in trouble. Silently, carefully, I managed to get inside, past the pigeon clocks and up the stairs, peeping quickly into the bar to see if anyone had raised the alarm. No. Good. I made it into the spare room, tore the lid off a storage carton and used it to stifle the gale that was now howling through the hole where the glass once was. I piled some of the many boxes against the window and, satisfied that no one would ever know, turned to leave. My exit was blocked by a little blond blackmailer — Dave! I wound up giving him my pocket money for six sad weeks to keep his mouth shut. It seems though that Dad knew about the window almost immediately, as well as the deal with Dave and figured it was punishment enough. I reckon I was very very lucky and that the local bloke had no idea how close he came to becoming a snow cone.

That pub is the source of many great memories. My Dad, who was a draughtsman, would travel every day to work in Birmingham and Mum would open the pub at six o'clock. While Mum made our supper I used to keep a discreet lookout for customers so she could pop out and tend the bar when needed, until Dad got home at around 6.30 p.m. and took over until closing. It was a great little team effort. I did my homework and changed the records on the player, then Dave and I would often go into the empty lounge and plink away at the piano, play darts or dominoes until tea was ready.

One day Dad declared we needed to call in the pest exterminators. I asked if we had rats, or mice or something, and he explained that he figured we had termites because the lounge wall was peppered with holes. 'It's the darndest thing,' he said, 'they are behind the leather sofas, just under the dartboard!' I went to the lounge and when I looked at the wall I realised the darts game Dave and I played was going to bring us big trouble. We used to play a version of 'chicken' with the darts, where one of us would stand or sit against the wall and try not to move as the other threw darts at the wall around us. My heart sank. When Dad found out those were not termite but dart holes we were going to be killed. I never did admit to causing a termite plague and I don't recall Dad calling in the exterminator. Miraculously the bugs seemed to stop making holes in the wall, and Dave must have felt as much to blame since, at least on this occasion, he didn't try to blackmail me.

When I was 12 my parents decided that to get a better education for Dave and me we needed to leave England. They considered Canada, but as we had relatives living in New Zealand we moved to the other side of the world, to the Land of the Long White Cloud. How exciting this was for two youngsters who until then had travelled no further than the seaside on holidays once a year. The day arrived, we drove to London, all of us chattering away nervously, Dave and me full of questions. My precious bike, along with everything we owned, had been packed into tea-chests and sent ahead of us but was not due to arrive for three weeks. We boarded our BOAC Comet 4 and belted in for a 52-hour flight with no stop-offs. I had been suffering an ear infection, which left me with an abscess in my left ear. I had to endure some 16 take-offs and landings on that journey and at times I thought my head was going to explode with the pain. Two weeks after the trip my ear drum perforated and even now, although flying is no problem, I can't dive any deeper than a swimming pool without trouble.

We visited so many exotic and fantastic-looking places on that adventure, even if we only observed them from the air or transit lounges. I could still say that, at the age of 12, I had been to Paris, where I tried to convince Dad to buy me some of those sunglasses that all the 'big stars' wore, and to Baghdad, Jakarta, Singapore, Delhi and so on. We arrived in Auckland and were whisked away to a small town called Otorohanga — try saying that with a Pommie twang. We were told we were heading to Thames and confusion set in. We tried to argue that our relatives must have been pronouncing it incorrectly. How could it possibly be the same as the great river back home? It felt to us as though the world had stopped when we moved to Thames. This was a truly beautiful seaside paradise but so quiet and untouched by the harsh realities we'd seen in England. There we were, two little, white, Pommie kids in the middle of February, floating on a rotten log in the water off Thames under the blazing sun. Bliss — what could go wrong? Sunstroke, that's what. We were forced to lie flat on our bilious stomachs for three days with our backs on fire and covered with blisters. As if that were not enough, our poor little chests and bellies were covered with bites from the bugs that were living in the rotten log.

Having learnt our lesson we settled in for an enjoyable six months or so in Thames. I joined the Sea Scouts and the Air Training Corp, as I had been a Scout in England. We went to school, fished a lot and rummaged at the rubbish dump, which used to be a popular pastime. You could easily spot the Brits at the tip because they were the ones wearing ties — I'm not joking! One very productive day, Dave and I collected bike parts and lawn-mower bits and pram wheels at the dump and dragged them for miles all the way home. We dropped the lot on the front lawn and went inside, exhausted, for a drink. When Dad went out to mow the lawn the nice bloke from across the street said, 'John, you could have saved us a trip to the dump if we'd known you wanted that stuff.' It turned out they'd just that morning dumped the pram wheels, the old bike and the lawn mower. Dad was not amused and neither were we.

We moved to Auckland next, and I was enrolled at Mount Albert Grammar School. I lasted three weeks. I'm not sure whether it was because it reminded me of my school days in England, or because it was a 'boys only' school, but I wasn't happy. I changed to Avondale College, and although it was a bit further from home I was a much happier chap. During these early days I didn't do much singing, preferring to hang out with the lads. They were very important years and it was during this time, I met my good friend Tony Rundle, whom even today, so many years later, I still count among my closest.

I painted my first car with Tony. We painted it by hand, me with the traditional four-inch brush. Actually, it wasn't even my car, but a borrowed one; but when we had finished the car was black with a white racing stripe. I invited Mum and Dad to take a ride with me into the city in this flash-looking car. The poor things — the car stank of petrol fumes and after three attempts to charge up the Farmers department store car-park ramp I had to ask them to get out to lighten the load! Luckily they laughed.

One of my first singing jobs came out of nowhere. I was taking dance lessons in Avondale College — a great way to meet the opposite sex. The school used to hold dances regularly on Friday nights, I guess to allow us to try out all our newly acquired dance skills. The Monkees were at the top of the charts at the time and one Friday someone handed me a microphone and said, 'Why don't you sing with the record?' So I sang along with Davey Jones that first time and everyone else that had made the charts. It became a feature of the Friday night dances. That was my first regular gig and I guess even though it was unpaid it was the start of my singing career. I loved my time at Avondale College. It was good to me and indeed for me. From time to time I still hear from Collegians past and current and it seems Avondale is as popular as ever. I have been invited to present the occasional award on prize days but unfortunately my schedule hasn't yet permitted that, though I would love to get there one day.

Geoff Sinclair, who went on to be prominent in radio, was a teacher at Avondale. On the day of my first Avondale cross-country race, under the eagle-eyed supervision of our teachers positioned around the course, I managed to catch Mr Sinclair's eye. I was the new kid and I'd kept a fairly low profile until then. The truth is I used to be quite good at cross-country and in England I'd won my Scouts' area competition. So, when I ran past Geoff ahead of the pack he called out to me, 'Boy, what is your name?' I called back, not missing a step, 'Guest, Sir'. He sternly retorted, 'I will not guess boy! What is your name?' We have since had many chances to laugh at this on and off the air. I'm sure he still thinks of me as that cheeky new kid who led the cross-country, though sadly I was beaten in the end.

One day out of the blue, Dad asked the family, 'What do you think of going to Canada?' We knew Mum and Dad had contemplated this earlier, but never realised they were serious. Dave and I were shocked! Before we knew it we had sold up and were on a P&O ship, the *Iberia*, bound for Vancouver. We had a wonderful crossing, visiting Suva and San Francisco on the way.

We found our new school amazingly free. Nothing strict, no uniforms, no need to worry if you missed a class, you could always 'make it up'. Nothing like what we were used to at all, and while Mum settled in quite well and began work as a cosmetician, Dad was not so happy. It seemed he was 'overqualified' for all the positions for which he applied. We were there at the beginning of the Vietnam War and at the time Canadians were only hiring other Canadians. It was very hard on Dad. He applied for new positions every day, only to be knocked back each time.

I had managed to get a job a couple of kilometres away from home. In the cold Canadian winter, I used to trudge out in the morning to put up trailer-type caravans and return after school to dismantle them before walking home again. It was like a car lot for campers and a very grounding experience for me. During this time I started my first band called The Apparition (no *Phantom* jokes please). We performed at pool parties and school dances and, in the short period we were there, we gained quite a following. The band, and my 'foreign' accent, made it quite easy for me to make friends so it was rather tough when Mum and Dad decided we would return to New Zealand.

Our 12-month stay in Canada seemed short but we all learned so much in that time. Travel is a wonderful eye-opener, and we saw different ways of life, different attitudes. It gave me the confidence to walk boldly into any situation without any sense of inferiority or inadequacy. From that time, I have never truly feared the unknown, which is a tremendous advantage in my career. So, we were shipboard again. This time the *Orsova* was taking us back to Auckland, via Hawaii and Fiji. It was another fabulous, though stormy, crossing. I managed to strike up a friendship with a bunch of people my age on board, some of whom played instruments. With the help of the ship's band we put together a group and entertained the passengers for the remainder of the cruise, which was great fun.

2.
A Shore Thing

BY THE TIME WE arrived in Auckland I was convinced that music had to take priority in my life. I told my parents I wanted to leave school — after all, I had already attended 13 of them. This is where life as I love it really began.

I looked for a band to join and auditioned for a group who at the time were doing very well and were at the top of the Auckland music scene. The band was called The Challenge and the late Benny Levin managed them. This time high hopes and hard work didn't pay off, but I was not daunted and continued to search for the right band.

I rehearsed with lots of musicians but nothing gelled. Then one day I answered an advertisement for a singer for a North Shore band called The Shore Thing. We worked together and a partnership was formed for a covers band playing hits. We needed transport for our gear, and I needed a job, so I went back to poring over the newspapers. This is how I got my first full-time job, as a van driver for a fashion house. It didn't pay so well but the job did come with a van and the business owners were lovely — so the band had transport! The Shore Thing entered the Coca-Cola Battle of the Bands as rank outsiders, but with a fantastic support team behind us we managed to make it through to the semi-finals. We decided we needed a less parochial name and my father suggested we should use the name of the band I had formed in Canada, so The Apparition lived again.

We toured and played at everything from 21st birthdays and weddings to surf-side booze-ups and dance parties. Most were good fun times but some of those gigs I'd rather forget — such as the evening we were booked to play for a surf club at their party. Everything was perfect until some over-zealous surf 'clubbies' generated an all-out brawl over a fickle girlfriend. I do believe we were lucky to get away from that one with our lives. Feeling as if our band career wasn't progressing quickly enough, that we needed to record at least one single, but without the means to do so, I wangled my way into a job as a packer at what was then Pye Records. Within three months I was working as stock controller and within six months was on the selection committee for new talent. I had just the talent in mind and guess who made a demo! The bigwigs at Pye liked what they heard enough to release 'It Must Be Love' by The Apparition. The single did so well it went through the roof and up to No. 2 on the Auckland hit chart, especially once Peter Sinclair (then on radio 1ZB) started to plug it. We were on our way!

We followed 'It Must Be Love' with another Top 10 hit called 'Justine', one of the first songs to use phasing. For the uninitiated, basically this is where a pair of tapes are slowed down and sped up to generate new sounds and variations to the music. This was so new at the time that it was both exciting and really very difficult. It drew on everyone's patience but the effect was worth the effort.

That year we developed a huge following and when the Battle of the Bands came around again we were ready, or so we thought, to take it on. Unfortunately, the members of the band were not always in agreement over the material. Our keyboard player loved bubble gum, the drummer was a soul man, our guitarist loved Traffic and Cream and the bass player was a Beatles fan. I was more into Three Dog Night and Deep Purple. This never usually presented a problem because we covered all tastes, but for the Battle of the Bands we had to choose one style and we could not seem to agree on anything. We began to notice the rift between us widening but we made a hasty choice and unfortunately lost our drummer just before the Battle. We still managed to secure second place regionally for Auckland, but not content with that, we re-entered in the Bay of Plenty area and won. We had made it into the National Finals. Having studied our competition we knew we had our work well and truly cut out. Craig Scott had told me about a band from Dunedin, called The Inbetweens. He'd said they were awesome and they certainly were. We fought it out with them in the Battle of the Bands National Final and lost. We had given it our best shot but they were incredible.

We continued playing our regular gig at Rangitoto College on Friday nights but the rot had begun to set in. It's really hard to keep five guys together and happy. I tip my hat to any band that can manage to stick together for more than a couple of years. Personalities get in the way. I was thrilled when we took a job for the 1970 Christmas season in Mount Maunganui because we were to share the billing with Reggie Ruka and the Classic Affair, in my opinion one of the best bands of the day. All was going well until I received a message from Benny Levin, who was still managing The Inbetweens, to ask me if I would be interested in joining them as front man because their singer had left. When I called the band together I think we all finally realised we were not unhappy about calling it a day. Each of us was dancing to a different tune by then and they gave me their blessing to move on. I took time to talk separately with each of the band members to be sure they were happy with our decision and, though I was concerned about letting our loyal fans down, I eventually made up my mind to leave. I had 30 songs to master before The Inbetweens' next job, plus we had a record to make. The time had come to get serious and so I left the security of my job at the record company. I remember that, having paid for petrol, the road crew and agent's fees, our first job actually earned us the grand sum of $8 for each show. Now that hurt!

Most people have very little idea of what show business entails and perhaps this is the way we like it. We understand that a little bit of mystery and a good dash of illusion are what help to maintain public interest. Each of us in the entertainment world creates an image for ourselves to suit that part of the industry we're involved in, whether we're aware of it or not and whether we like it or not. In my early rock'n'roll days it was mandatory to have shoulder-length hair (or longer) and we made an individual statement with the colour. Mine was an outrageous plum red which looked great at night in a smoke-filled room under lights, but I looked a shocker in the daylight. I also wore the compulsory tight leather pants, high-heeled shoes and shirt unbuttoned to the navel. That's the problem with having been in the music industry for as long as I have. All those dreadful fashion choices we make come back to haunt us. Just the image of that rock'n'roll animal I've outlined makes me both laugh . . . and cringe. I'm sure you can see that, as the biggest rock 'n' roll act in the country, having made numerous television appearances and a few Top 10 records, we could not afford to let our audience know we earned only $8 a show.

This would have surely burst our bubble, trashed our illusion, ruined our image.

So, The Inbetweens had a new vocalist and life was grand. Nothing could beat being a pop star and performing on stage. We had a ball, though we never knew where our next meal was coming from, often landing at my folks' door for a good home-cooked supper. We were having tremendous fun but there was absolutely no security. The major prize in the Battle of the Bands was a deal to play a line-up of bookings at various clubs in Sydney. An incredible opportunity, but we just couldn't work out how we'd pay for ourselves to get there and then to live. So we took advantage of every single opportunity to earn before we went, playing 21st birthdays, weddings, surf club socials and bikie reunions — you name it, we played it.

Our poor old Bedford van was on its way out, coupled up to a trailer which Dad had made at work for The Apparition's Christmas tour just a couple of months earlier. With six guys aboard and all that gear we had to lug around it barely rolled down a hill, never mind breaking any speed limits. On the way back to Auckland from Whangarei we all had to pitch in to get the old truck around the corners. We all knew the drill — as each bend approached everyone had to drop their magazines, pies and music sheets, hold the gear in place and pray we made the bend intact as Murray and I wrestled with the steering wheel. This was well before the days of power steering anyway, but our old tourer's steering had just about seized completely. On $8 a week the repair was going to have to wait, as were the tyres which had been around New Zealand a few too many times already. The suspension of our much-loved trailer was never designed to carry the ridiculous load we imposed upon it. Whenever we hit a pothole the trailer would 'bottom out' with such force it would lift the van's rear end into the air. During that brief moment of lift the van steered like it was riding on air — almost like having power steering.

Those early days of touring were exhausting but heaps of fun. A practical joker of some repute, I was in my element, with so many opportunities. A particularly easy target was Noddy, our ever-exhausted roadie (no, I can't tell you why we called him that!). This poor guy was paid $10 a week by each of us in the band to set up, carry around and maintain our equipment, no matter how many shows we did. One night we headed out of Gisborne, after we finished our four-hour show at midnight and Noddy had packed everything into the van and trailer while we got something to eat (as usual). We were on the road by 1.30 a.m. since we had to be back the following afternoon in reasonable condition for a TV appearance in Auckland. About an hour into our journey Noddy declared he needed a toilet stop. Now, I'm the kind of driver who thinks breaks are a nuisance and likes a good uninterrupted trip, and I knew if I woke the snoring band by stopping they'd probably all want to get out for something to eat and waste another hour of our time.

But Noddy was insistent. 'Ro-o-o-ob mate, I reeaaally need to go!' When Noddy's pitiful whining finally managed to wake Murray who was sitting on the front seat, Murray and I exchanged a conspiratorial glance. I pulled to a halt as Noddy breathed a sigh of relief and leapt out the door. As he leapt I whispered to him that I had to move the van off the road but he was preoccupied and paid me no attention. We cruised along slowly for about 300 m, pulled off the road, woke the boys and told them of our plan. While poor Noddy was relieving himself we hopped out and walked back in the pitch dark towards where we'd left him and hid in the bushes. After a moment or two we heard Noddy chattering to himself about what he planned to do to us for making him walk so far back to the van. As he went past us we leapt from the dark wailing like lunatics, sending Noddy screaming into the night. Man, could he jump! We laughed all the way to Hamilton.

Life was moving so quickly at this stage that it all seems a blur. The memory of each show runs into the next as I recall touring New Zealand from north to south and back again. We worked non-stop for almost 12 months in preparation for our move to Australia. Benny, our manager, was a bit of a smooth operator and did a deal with an Italian shipping company for our trip to Sydney. No three-hour flight for us but five luxurious days cruising the Pacific on the *Achille Lauro* (it was later hijacked). So, we hauled our gear down to Princes Wharf in Auckland and lugged it aboard the ship. I remember this departure so vividly. We lined the deck waving goodbye to friends and family with such emotion and excitement you'd have thought we were heading off to another galaxy instead of crossing the Tasman. It was not the luxury vessel Benny had made it out to be, but life on board was just fine. I have to mention here that Paul, our crazy drummer, got completely carried away with this international cruising idea. He announced to us all, with great pride, that he'd changed all his money to *lire*. Yes, *lire*. We had to explain that we were only on the ship for five days, and he had no answer to how he planned to spend his lire in Sydney.

We made an inauspicious landing — we responded to a paging for five musicians only to be told they were looking for the English group Marmalade. We waited until the rest of the passengers had disembarked before we unloaded our gear onto pallets and headed to the customs shed. There we sat for eight long, boring hours while our equipment was taken completely to pieces. Every screw was removed from the speaker boxes, our talcum powder was tasted, Paul was strip-searched — probably because he was cheeky — and all the time we waited and watched for a friendly face to rescue us. Finally, just as all our luggage was cleared, our contact showed up and whisked us away to Bondi and the flat that was to be our home for the next twelve months. In the apartment block next door was another New Zealand band, The High Revving Tongues. We immediately felt right at home and, once we'd all established that none of us would share a room with Paul, we each found our corner in the three-bedroom apartment.

We had been hired to work the club circuit and were ready to take up our Sydney contracts at Whiskey a Go Go, Chequers and The Stagecoach etc. Once we got going, we were playing every night except Sundays from 7.30 p.m. through to 3 a.m. Sometimes we had the luxury of 20-minute sets, alternating with another band — and what a line-up they were too. Some of the best and most popular bands in Australia worked the circuit, including Sherbet, Harry Young and Sabbath, and Autumn, and they made us sound somewhat inferior. We were forced to take a good look at our equipment and realised we needed a new PA. I purchased a new system on tick and, while it set me back most of my savings, at least we were competitive. When you are working these long hours and screaming your lungs out night after night doing Led Zeppelin, Deep Purple and Three Dog Night covers, something has to give. And it did. My voice just said ENOUGH and I lost my falsetto, then gradually my lower register. For a while I relied solely on a product called AAA throat spray, which would numb my throat and allow me to perform. I didn't know from one song to the next whether my voice was going to take an unplanned holiday.

Why didn't I stop, you may well ask. I could not let the guys down, there were four other wage-earners who depended on me, as I did on them, to get the job done; we could not perform without a complete group. Neither did it help matters that paying our bills left us without enough money to eat properly. I remember having to run a $2 tab at the corner store for a tray of sausages. I cringe to think I had to cross the road to dodge the store as I couldn't pay the bloke back. My parents sent me $20 for Christmas that year and when I opened the envelope I nearly cried. Never had I needed help so much — my voice was shot, I was down to under 10 stone in weight and I

Idol in the making

ALL EYES ON ROB

SOUND SCENE

SUNDAY STAR TIMES

IT is the era of the teenage pop idols. Britain has the outrageous Marc Bolan and America the clean-cut 22-year-old David Cassidy. Across the Tasman, the youthful Johnny Farnham reigns supreme.

In New Zealand newcomer 19-year-old Rob Guest is tipped to win adulation.

A resident on "Happen Inn", Rob is being groomed for pop stardom by Auckland agents Glenn Tabuteau and Lew Pryme.

They are convinced the 19-year-old North Shore singer can recapture the glory and esteem formerly showered on singers such as Johnny Devlin and Mr Lee Grant.

Adulation

"The time is ripe for another teenage heart throb," says Glenn Tabuteau. "Pop trends tend to revolve"

In the beginning we had Johnny Devlin and then nothing until Mr Lee Grant emerged in 1966.

"True we've had singers like Shane and Craig Scott since Lee's heyday but neither in all honesty have had that same magical quality.

"They really haven't been idols.

"Good performers yes: they haven't won true adulation. One only has to look overseas at present to see this new trend.

"In Britain there's mass hysteria over Marc Bolan, in the U.S. you have David Cassidy and Donny Osmond as teenage figureheads.

"The trend has to happen here and I'm sure Rob can be the one to win through.

"He's younger than his other pop competition and that's very important.

"Pop fans today want to identify with people their own age.

"They don't want favourites that older brothers and sisters may have swooned over."

It's planned

No other New Zealand pop performer has had the debut Rob Guest has had.

In seven days he has appeared on three top-rated national television programmes.

For the past eight weeks since his return from Sydney, where he worked with the Inbetweens, he has been kept "under wraps" by the Fuller's agency.

"This has been intentional," says Glenn Tabuteau. "Rob's year has been planned like a military operation.

"We wanted the TV shows to precede personal appearances.

Concerts

"Next thing is the hit record and producer Terry Condon together with arranger Bruce Lynch is sure he can come up trumps.

"When school resumes we will have Rob appearing in lunch-hour concerts along with the Rumour and Freeway.

"A series of 30-minute concerts have already been lined up for metropolitan colleges. I only hope we can repeat this format right through the country."

ROB GUEST . . . emerging from the wraps.

The more popular you become the more people have to pigeon-hole you — newspaper article from the 1970s.

---

was utterly broke. Disagreements began to fragment the band. We ran into problems with one of the organisers at one of the clubs and he effectively put us out of work for a week. It did mean that my voice got a much-needed rest but now we were in serious financial trouble. We decided to disband. Serendipitously, a letter arrived that very day from Benny. He said that the producers of the television series 'Happen Inn' wanted me to be resident singer for six weeks. I was going home, and I had work!

———

We sold all the gear at an incredible loss and went our separate ways. I have heard tales from time to time about the antics and activities of the other guys: Roland appeared on 'This is Your Life' for me and it was great to see him. I've lost track of Tony and Paul but sadly Murray passed away. He was a good mate and I will miss him greatly. All of a sudden it seemed I was a solo act. No longer did I have to consider the wishes of four other team-mates, but neither could I share with them the funny moments, achievements and failures. There was no one to answer to but also no one to blame.

When I arrived back in Auckland I went straight to see Benny and Russell Clarke. They were managing Craig Scott and Bunny Walters, whose careers had gone through the roof under their direction. I decided that I too needed representation, someone who would look after my interests because they believed in me. I spoke to Phil Warren, who had just sold Fullers Entertainment Bureau to a young guy called Lew Pryme. Lew was known to me as a pop singer in the days of 'C'mon', but we had never met, so I called him and we arranged to meet. We got along brilliantly and began what was to become a 19-year association. He not only became my manager but a very, very dear friend.

The 'Happen Inn' experience provided a great learning curve. Suddenly I had to walk, sing and play to the camera — a fair diversion in style for the ex-frontman of a rock 'n' roll band. We used to prerecord the vocals at Mascot Studios a week ahead of the show taping, then, under the guidance of Bernie Allen, Kevin Moore and John Barningham, I became a television performer. Who could have guessed at the time that this six-week stint would become a model for most of my career? I seriously suspect that without that willing, helpful and patient crew giving me a leg up into the industry the way they did, I would not be performing today. I had the most fantastic opportunity, an on-the-job apprenticeship where I was allowed to learn and hone my craft, especially learning what not to do as much as what worked.

It was during these days of transition between rock 'n' roll and television that I was to meet my first wife. Just saying it like that — 'first wife' — makes it sound as though it was doomed from the start, but this was not the case . . . we were to spend the next 16-odd years together, eight before we were married. Lynette was the principal dancer on 'Happen Inn' and was known for her long hair as well, of course, as her talent for dancing. I was watching a rehearsal, standing waiting for my number, which was next, when a mane of hair hit me in the face. I'm still not sure if this was deliberate, but knowing Lynette I doubt it — I was just in the way. So, we met. Over the next few weeks we began to date and the rest, as they say, is history.

I remember one evening after I had finished recording an episode of 'Happen Inn', I was in Palmerston North staying at the local pub. I wandered into the lounge at around 6 p.m. to watch the show on the television. As the show began, some kids and their parents came in but didn't give me a second glance as they settled in to watch. During the first commercial break one of the children spotted me. I'll never forget the look on her face as she looked from me to the screen and back — as the programme returned she became quite perplexed. How could I possibly be there watching the show with them and on the television at the same time?

Television has the ability to catapult a person's career by creating familiarity, by projecting you right into your audience's living rooms. In those days, television was truly variety-based, something I think is sadly missing today. Back then it gave many of us a chance to succeed. I was lucky to do many more residencies on 'Happen Inn' and sang a great range of songs from that time. What made it possible, of course, was that there were no video clips of the original performers as we have today.

As the popularity of the show continued to grow, other shows were launched in competition. I remember in particular 'Norman' and 'Popco', hosted by a very young and glittery Paul Holmes.

Opposite page: Studying a script at home, 1972. What's with the toilet paper cover poodle? Mum put it there to cheer up the room. Thanks Mum.

Publicity shot, 1973 — taken by Dad.

This was back when television in New Zealand was segmented into four regions: AKTV2 (Auckland), WNTV1 (Wellington), CHTV3 (Christchurch) and DNTV4 (Dunedin). Yes, even before TV2. At one stage I was approached to appear on 'Popco', which was Christchurch-based and previously only used local talent. So in one week I was on both shows, which opened up all sorts of possibilities; the market was now wide open, especially when 'Ready to Roll' started in Wellington at the then-new Avalon Studios. The competition among the regions was rife, which meant absolutely no shortage of work. At one time I was learning up to a dozen songs a week and flying backwards and forwards between the centres. Among these appearances all over the country I fitted in the occasional TV special, a few six-week series and 'Stars on Sunday'. I was becoming very well known and even appeared in Australia on the 'Ernie Sigley Show', taped in Wellington. All this television exposure brought interest from cabaret producers as well as recording opportunities. Lew and I decided it was probably time to get a little grounded again so we developed a series of lunchtime concerts for the schools in the Auckland region, mainly the girls' schools (yes this was purely a marketing decision!). We kept the shows very current and tied them to my television work by taking a band into the schools at lunchtimes and playing half a dozen songs from my TV playlist for that week.

I recall doing a show at Epsom Girls' Grammar School, and as usual the kids came onto the stage at the end of the show in search of autographs. Well, the girls only had an hour for lunch and the show ran over time, so when the autograph signing began some of the girls, in a bit of a hurry, started to push from the back of the crowd. By the time this push reached me it had become an incredible shove. I was launched off my platform shoes and backwards over a trapdoor or something in the stage, landing unflatteringly on my tush. The next day the press announced that I had been mobbed at a girls' school and the way they constructed the story made it sound like I'd been lucky to escape with my clothes. I should be so lucky! This episode did no harm to my image, but Lew and I did have a word or two about truth and the media. It is so easy to be misquoted, and no amount of truth will get in the way of a good story. A few weeks after this incident a Sunday paper carried a photo of me and pronounced that I was the New Zealand version of David Cassidy. He was hugely popular then and I have nothing against David Cassidy, but I had invested a fair effort into creating my niche in this ever-changing business. I was not thrilled with any comparison, but it was more positive publicity.

Recordings had started but the elusive smash hit just wouldn't happen. The songs we chose to record were all right but nothing was setting the world on fire. I was performing them on television but the radio stations were developing an aversion to local artists. The market had really opened up and the advertising dollar was flowing to those stations giving airplay to international artists. The choice for programmers between a Top 10 artist in the United Kingdom or the United States and a local artist without a number one hit was obvious. Now, don't get me wrong, the early records we produced did quite well. They usually made the Top 20, some even higher; it depended on the regional stations. If I had been to a centre it was reflected in our chart performance. This became very frustrating, as more and more travel became necessary.

Doubts began to creep into my mind about my career choices. Had I done the right thing? Should I have become a journalist, or the big bass drummer in the Salvation Army? As the music and television industries exploded with new technologies the world seemed to become one big market. It felt somehow as though I was marking time. I needed to keep up. I began dreaming of a phone call from Hollywood. I was always prepared to work for it, but I wanted those opportunities, I needed to sing, I needed to perform. During a break I'm fine for the first day or so, but I soon become twitchy and unbearable and then it's time for me to get on with what I do. Every day I called Lew. Every day he would tell me to be patient. When I watched the television shows I'd been on I'd begin to doubt myself and wonder why these other artists were up there performing instead of me. Was there a problem? Did we charge too much last time? At $60 a show for 'Happen Inn', including the time spent on rehearsals, recording and taping the show, less 20 per cent commissions, I was left the grand total of $48. I couldn't believe I was too expensive. I figured I would have been better off with the band. Even Noddy earned more than I did. That was the going rate though, no bargaining allowed. Take it or leave it — to the next up-and-coming, who *would* take it. Lew finally called and when he did, he spun the steering wheel of my career once again.

M TUBBERTY

3.
Enter Stage Right

IT TURNED OUT LEW had a call from a producer named William Forbes Hamilton, who was planning an exciting new musical production and wanted me to sing for them. Lew set up a meeting for me with director Dickie Johnson and the musical director Gary Daverne. I sang for them and they offered me the leading role of Jesus Christ in a production from Australia, which had been called *The Jesus Christ Revolution*. It was to open in Auckland entitled *Man of Sorrows*. I plunged excitedly into this project without any idea of where it would take me. Those days were wonderful, the process of rehearsing and experimenting and discovering was amazing. I loved being on stage and this thoroughly professional team had everything in its place and happening on cue.

I've often said that presenting a piece of good-quality theatre is like buying someone a very special present and watching them open it and sharing the joy. That is what it's all about for me. The chance to transport us all for a short time away from the everyday, humdrum, nine to five, the worry of paying bills and making lunches. To take the audience to a world where time stands still and they get to experience someone else's story. It's pure magic.

Man of Sorrows was a smash! With a fabulous cast including Grant Bridger as Judas, Elizabeth Hellawell as Mary Mother and Max Cryer as Pontius Pilate, it was supposed to run for only two weeks but it was still sold out six weeks later. Unhappily, we had to close because of 'lack of theatre availability', an expression I was to hear many times in the future. I was at a real loss when *Man of Sorrows* finished. I still made television appearances and recorded the odd track, but I had bigger fish to fry. I needed to find another stage production to satisfy my new hunger and I pestered Lew every day to help me find one. As it happened, it found me.

Robert Young, who had been assistant choreographer and a dancer on 'Happen Inn', was now directing theatre shows. He had called Lew because he was working with the Hamilton Operatic Society and about to direct *Joseph and the Amazing Technicolor Dreamcoat*. He wanted me to play Joseph, and explained that although the society didn't normally use professionals in their productions, he'd managed to convince them to consider me. I had not heard of the show, but a little research revealed that it had started life as a 15-minute school production — quite a transformation!

Opposite page: Grant Bridger as Judas (left), me as Jesus in *Man of Sorrows*, Auckland, 1973.

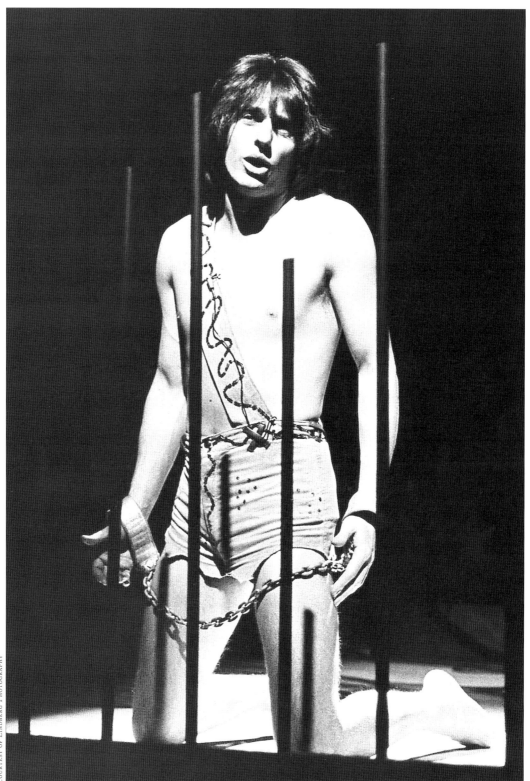

Opposite page: Behind bars, as Joseph in *Joseph and the Amazing Technicolor Dreamcoat* singing 'Close Every Door'.

Left: Joseph, the Baker and Butler — Rotorua, 1975.

It was by two fairly new writers, Andrew Lloyd Webber and Tim Rice . . . wonder what ever happened to them . . . tee-hee. The songs, such as 'Any Dream Will Do' and 'Close Every Door' were contagious, the atmosphere was wonderful and the show was terrific fun — even though the costume was a little skimpy. Very early in the piece, I discovered a product called Sudden Tan and I used BUCKETS of it. The only problem with using it as often as I had to was the grubby look it gave to my ankles, knees and wrists. Oh well, that's showbiz.

Robert always had such great ideas and knew how to bring them to life. He brought out the best in me and created a sell-out show from a virtually unknown musical. I had the good fortune to do many other shows with Robert including *Half a Sixpence*, *Jesus Christ Superstar*, *Barnum* and even return seasons of *Joseph*. He will always be a dear friend and I admire him enormously. I just hope that one day we will get to do another show together. I owe that man so very, very much.

The success of *Joseph* in Hamilton generated interest in many other regions and before I knew it I was playing *Joseph* everywhere. It was always a sell-out and, with a cast of thousands, everyone had a ball. To this day I still get messages from people in those audiences which usually start with, 'I was in the choir with you in *Joseph* in Hamilton or Rotorua or somewhere. I'm sure you won't remember me, I was ten at the time. I'm married now with three children'. Now, how old does that make me feel, though I guess I should be happy they're not grandparents yet! Usually, I'm very good at remembering faces; it's names that give me a hard time. Occasionally people I've met, maybe once, will become upset if I don't recognise them. This is a no-win situation. If they start with, 'You don't remember me, do you?' and I say reservedly, 'Yes I do' (because I DO recall faces), they will retort, 'Well, what's my name?' Uh-oh! And if I say no, they get offended. People have asked me whether I mind requests for autographs when I'm out, say at a restaurant, but that has never bothered me at all. Most people are very thoughtful, give me space and choose moments to catch my attention. I firmly believe you have no business being in the public eye if you can't talk to the people who put you there.

So, now I had my television, theatre shows, cabaret and recording, but somehow this was still not enough. It seemed like feast or famine, either frantically learning new material or sitting around

Visiting some lovely
people with Iris during
Joseph season, Balclutha.

with nothing to do. The seasons were not very long and even though I was doing half a dozen productions a year, I still had time on my hands. So I was back on the phone to Lew. It may sound as though I was never happy, but that's not the reality. If I was involved in a production, either on television or stage, then I was involved boots and all and time really had no relevance. My perspective was skewed by my insatiable appetite for the stage.

In 1976 I was invited to work in Australia again, the first time since the days of The Inbetweens. My contract was for a daily 20-minute set over one month at the prestigious South Sydney Juniors Club and I was to share the bill with a British act, The Morton Frasier Harmonica Gang. I was to perform with a larger band than usual, conducted by Lionel Huntingdon, so I needed someone to arrange and score my music. I contacted Mike Harvey, whom I had met at the Station Hotel where I had been performing in cabaret. This venue was probably the best of its kind in Auckland and Salty Dog, Mike's band, was undoubtedly top-shelf.

When I arrived in Sydney I went into rehearsal with only the rhythm charts for some of the songs, as Mike was burning the midnight oil to get the rest finished. I remember the musos at the club being unimpressed with this young Kiwi upstart without full arrangements. Lionel's advice to me at the time was to put in a couple of standards. He suggested a few songs, including 'Danny Boy', but I didn't know the words. Lew kindly wrote them out for me on a beer coaster and I sang it that night. Phew — it brought the house down. In those days, club management judged the success of your performance by the number of people who stopped playing the pokies during your act — a rule I'm glad I don't have to go by today. Anyway, Mike got the arrangements to me as promised and the shows must have gone down well as I was invited back to Sydney to perform at some of the other major clubs. I really cut my teeth on the Sydney club circuit. Ten in the morning on a Sunday wake-up show, when everyone was a little under the weather was not the easiest place to produce that gentle, warm tone one needs to deliver a convincing love song. The audiences were lovely though, and I learned a heap. I couldn't believe that I had to do a 20-minute set, not 19 (and a bit) and not 21 (heaven forbid) and NO GAGS. ('If we wanted a comedian, we'd have booked one . . . Just sing!') I could have done that with my hands tied behind my back, but they were the ones with the cheque-book.

Back in New Zealand, Robert Young had a new venture and once again it seemed he was looking for me. Robert and Lew had organised for me to recreate a role made famous by Tommy Steele, that of Arthur Kipps, a cheeky Cockney known as Artie in *Half a Sixpence*. This Kipps character was very naive but you couldn't help liking him. This one was right up my alley and, unlike *Joseph*, this part had dialogue as well as song. Watching the movie I realised that I wasn't just to sing and act but I had to dance. Not just any dancing either, I had just six weeks to learn how to tap-dance and play the banjo! So, I crossed back over the Tasman and took up tap-dancing lessons. Every morning I went to dance lessons, each afternoon I worked with Robert and also learned to play a banjo. From 7 p.m. every day I had to gather what I had learned and try to put it together with the company in Hamilton, who had already been rehearsing for six months. Everyone was so supportive and I knew a lot of the cast from *Joseph* so the team melded together well and the show, as they say, went on.

The rhythm of a show runs deeper than the musical score — it is the essence which captures an audience. When it's there, it's poetry in motion; when it's not there, the show closes soon after opening. This rhythm cast its spell in *Sixpence* and it showed in the queue for tickets, which wrapped itself around Founders Theatre each night. Having said all was well is not entirely true. I'm sure you've heard that in television and theatre it's never good to work with children or animals. I can personally confirm that at least half the theory is spot on.

Act I, scene one, *Sixpence*, Hamilton . . . Artie Kipps is meant to appear through a shop counter, carrying Edwin, the shop cat, a friendly moggy supplied by one of the backstage team. Every night my co-star would arrive at my dressing room, where I would have a saucer of milk and a can of cat food ready and waiting. We were the best of mates all through rehearsals. Opening night did not even give him the jitters. But one night, the inevitable happened: Edwin wandered off and could not be found. Fortunately, his job description was simply that he had to be grossly overweight and he had to look overfed. The adept crew found a rotund alternative just in time. They stuffed us together under the counter-top and I delivered my opening line: 'Good morning, Edwin'. Well, that cat went ballistic, there were claws and arms everywhere. A high-pitched squeal reverberated through the theatre. I believe it was mine. I was acutely aware that 2000 people were watching this cat lacerate me under very bright lights — and with an orchestra playing — as it struggled to free itself of my grasp. There was blood everywhere by the time I gave up and dropped this Rambo with fur (I was kindly told later that even at home he wouldn't let himself be picked up unless he wanted to. THANKS.) He settled calmly, mid-stage, and preened. And preened. And preened. Edwin was eventually lured off stage and into the wings by a very anxious crew and the show continued, with me bleeding from multiple puncture wounds. A little before halfway through the show I became aware of a titter in the audience. I had absolutely no idea why they might be giggling until I saw Edwin preening centre-stage. Apparently he'd managed to dodge or shred the many coaxing hands in the wings and had second thoughts about his 15 minutes of fame. I must say it was a job and a half to resume control of the stage! Thankfully the original cat did return and I think I would have fed it caviar and cream each night if I could have heard it promise not to run away again.

I never claimed to be a dancer, but I am able to move and create the illusion that I know what I'm doing. It takes years of practice to learn how to make it look easy, but I hoped my four-week crash course would help me to fake it. I needed to 'be' Sammy Davis Jnr for one number at least. Some very clever choreography, working around my limited skills, had even me believing that I wasn't bad. The audience, I'm glad to say, believed my performance as well. The illusion was not so easy to maintain with the banjo playing though. I had figured that if I tuned the banjo the way one tunes a guitar, an instrument I am familiar with, then I could play it on stage and look competent. The banjo player in the orchestra pit was to make the music for me, but it was important that my playing looked and sounded reasonable too.

On the occasion I recall, the cast had thrown me my banjo; I'd plucked it from the air on cue and started to strum but the strings were totally slack and the sound was horrible. As I became entangled in the strings I realised that the bridge, which holds the strings firm, had collapsed in the throw to me and I could do nothing about it. Luckily the guy in the pit played a mean banjo and the audience heard a great banjo fill anyway, but the illusion was shot. On another occasion of banjo madness, thankfully much later in the season, I was glad of all the time and practice. As I glanced into the pit I realised in horror that the chap who was to play my piece as I mimed had broken a string on his banjo, and I had to play the part on my own. I'm afraid I had so much fun that the banjo player in the pit became redundant, at least for one song, and I played for real from that moment on.

Half a Sixpence was a very energetic show! Along with all that dancing and banjo playing I also had to perform some clowning stunts. I never would have thought I'd need to learn how to fall over chairs or hang from lamp-posts. I loved the comedy aspect to the show and it took all my self-control each night, with the audience laughing raucously, not to digress from the script. It's amazingly seductive, you want to give them that pleasure again and stretch the moment as far as possible. The Hamilton season was a sell-out and other centres picked up on this and booked me to play Kipps again and again. The beautiful thing about this, truly, was the variety of directing and choreographic styles. It was a fresh production everywhere we went, with new people, new routines to familiar songs, and subtle or not so subtle changes to stage arrangements. When we played *Sixpence* in New Plymouth, the director added a touch to the tap number that was so cute it brought the house down. They had arranged for two little local tap-dancing lads to shadow me as I crossed from one wing to the other. As I disappeared and reappeared again these mini-mes, in identical costume, would turn and turn about and follow me across the stage, mimicking all the moves perfectly. These guys, who were around eight years old sure knew how to tap, in fact I recall they were New Zealand champions. I also recall having to pick up these kids, one under each arm, and carry them to their dressing rooms after the curtain calls, partly because the incessant tapping of their little feet would drive me and the crew crazy. The show was doing really well, everyone was happy, then one day I heard a little voice saying, 'Mr Guest, can I give you some advice? You must lift your heels when you tap.' So much for faking it, these kids were perfectionists. I made them walk back to their dressing rooms after that. What was it I said before about kids and animals . . . ? No, really, they were terrific kids.

I learned to become independent of the company (as often I was the only one who had done this show before) and at the same time maintain my part in the all-important teamwork. When I play these roles, my name may appear above the title, but I know that I am only as good as the company, and we all work together to create the impression that stays with an audience . . . the cast member with one line, the person who clears lolly wrappers after a show. Everyone is appreciated.

Practical jokes are great fun, I should know! The stage, however, is no place to play tricks since the joke can easily get right out of control. One *Sixpence* performance taught me a great lesson. My character Kipps gets drunk in a scene where he scoffs a yard of ale. This glass was regularly filled

Opposite page: Publicity shot Jesus Christ and Mary Magdalene — *Jesus Christ Superstar,* Rotorua, 1970s.

The Last Supper —
Superstar, 1979.

KERRY GRANT PHOTOGRAPHY, ROTORUA

with flat ginger ale, yuk, or cold tea, double yuk! Cheered on by the crowd on stage, Kipps downs the 'ale'. I always took pride in my attempts to make it look real, so I would gulp down as much as possible. On this particular occasion, on cue, I tipped the yard and began to gulp what turned out to be straight scotch! The shock on my face must have been a picture, but what was going on in my head was not pretty. My lesson — never, ever, ever drink anything on stage without smelling it first. The rest of that show went surprisingly quickly and by the time we took our bows I was feeling no pain. I never did find out who was responsible — and such lousy scotch too. Could it have been my understudy? Naughty thoughts, Rob, very unkind . . .

As my first role in live theatre was Jesus in *Man of Sorrows* it was very interesting to be offered the role of Jesus again, in *Jesus Christ Superstar*. There were so many questions in my mind: primarily, would I be able to play the same character differently because of the interpretation placed upon it by the structure of the show? Playing Jesus was a daunting prospect, calling into question my personal stand on religion, something I knew I had to put aside entirely to be impartial for the role. I was also aware that for so many people this production meant so much, and that for different groups it held different kinds of significance. It was important to realise that half my audience might be believers, while the other might not. This was going to have to be a very well-planned treading of the boards, but I was bound to tread on some toes no matter how carefully I played this complicated role. The mail that arrived attested to the variety of zealots out there. I received everything from crucifixes to letters claiming the world was about to end. I had to wonder about these people. This all happened in 1974 and, as far as I can tell, life as we know it ain't changed much. How did these bearers of cataclysmic tidings feel about themselves the day after the world didn't implode? Perhaps they found a new cause, or switched to a career in politics. All that aside, playing Jesus in that production was a wonderful experience. It was only my second Andrew Lloyd Webber show and I had no idea at the time how great a role this man was to play, indirectly, in my future career.

Backstage at the Dunes Hotel, Las Vegas, backstage 1980, with Caesar the lion. Don't let the smile fool you — mine I mean.

Right: Mike and myself backstage, Song for the Pacific. Mike's song 'Hangin' On' won this inaugural contest, then competed in the Pacific Song Contest (complicated huh!)

Below: With United States songwriter, David Livingstone, and Mike Harvey — Pacific Song Contest, 1978.

ROB GUEST COLLECTION

ROB GUEST COLLECTION

On stage at Harrah's Hotel, Atlantic City, in *Steppin' Out*, singing Peter Allen's 'Rio', 1981.

AMDRAM PRESENTATION OF *BARNUM*, WANGANUI, 1986 DIRECTED BY ROBERT YOUNG.

Publicity flyer for *Barnum*.

With Peter Turner and Jude, *Barnum*, 1987 — at the Regent Theatre, Dunedin.
It was Peter who set himself on fire.

Kawerau — *Grease*, backstage after the final curtain. That's me on the far left.

Playing Danny Zuko in *Grease*, with the T-birds.

Right: A shed, or what's left of one, after the earthquake in Edgecumbe.

Below: With the crew of *Grease*, known fondly as 'The Dirt'. Craig Pilkinton is in the second row with the pale blue shirt — trouble!

ROB GUEST COLLECTION

ROB GUEST COLLECTION

4.
On the Road

IT WAS NOW 1976–77 and I continued with cabaret, though only about once a fortnight. *Joseph* was starting up in new centres everywhere, so I was performing from Cape Reinga to Bluff, with an enormous amount of travelling. Television and recording took up what was left of my time but I was still keen to find another theatre show. It occurred to me at this point that I was in danger of being typecast, at least as far as stage performance was concerned. I had performed in three major, religion-based shows: *Man of Sorrows*, *Joseph* and *Superstar*, and I needed to choose my next production very carefully.

When Lew called, it was with great news. The Mercury Theatre in Auckland were going to produce *Pippin*, and yes, they wanted me to play the lead. I love this aspect of show business — just when life begins to feel a little routine, the whole deck of cards can fly into the air on a phone call.

Around this time I was actually very busy; I had just recorded 'Hangin' On', a wonderful up-tempo song composed by my dear friend Mike Harvey, and it had gone through the roof. I was planning an album, performing

ROB GUEST COLLECTION

In full flight — during a performance in Auckland.

RCB GUEST COLLECTION

When did my infatuation with the automobile begin? Posing with someone else's baby, England.

Joseph in Tauranga and 'Hangin' On' had been selected to represent New Zealand in the inaugural Pacific Song Contest. That same week I was made Entertainer of the Year — my feet were not on the ground!

Rehearsals for *Pippin* were from 10 a.m. until 4 p.m. in Auckland. I would then have to get into the car and drive the 150 km to Tauranga, perform *Joseph* and when finished drive back to Auckland to get a few hours' sleep before having to rehearse again at 10 a.m. Lew kept saying, 'Don't worry, Robbie. It's only for two weeks, you'll be fine.' So I decided he needed to share the experience and insisted he travel with me, to 'keep me company, and safe'. Back and forth, we travelled together, in my Mach 1 Mustang, a big, powerful gas-guzzler with left-hand drive. After the first week fatigue was affecting us both. Lew dealt with it by talking — non-stop. Yak, yak, yak! The only way I could shut him up was to swing our big car out into the right-hand lane and overtake whenever we came up behind someone slower than us. He nearly had a heart attack so many, many times because he never realised that I could see, on the inside of the vehicle in front, that the road was clear. I never bothered to enlighten him . . . would I be that unkind to an old mate? You betcha!

Cars, as you might have guessed, are my other passion. In 1974 I bought a new, blue Ford Capri 3000GT, one of the first Series II in the country. This was a beautiful car and I enjoyed many thousands of kilometres of perfectly wonderful motoring until, on a drive from Auckland to Wellington, the thrust bearing in the clutch started to moan. By the time I reached Wellington the noise was almost unbearable. That Capri and I had travelled 20,000 km over that year but Wellington was the end of the line. I was there for a week of cabaret and it turned out I would finally get a chance to take a proper look at that silver Monaro GTS I'd spotted in the car yard.

Between rehearsals and working each night I had not had a chance to get to the yard, and when I did get there, of course, it had been sold. Now, we all know the feeling, when something you've had your heart set on suddenly becomes unavailable. This is how I felt about that car. Why? I don't know. I tried to get the name of the buyer with the intention of talking them into selling it to me. But it was not to be. The dealer did manage to get me a Monaro LS with electric everything and in wonderful condition. Wasting no time I traded the Capri and bought myself the 'Monee'. This was ridiculous — sometimes I question my sanity — the Monaro, a big V8, chewed through fuel, and we were on petrol rationing in New Zealand at the time. In order to get from Wellington to Auckland I had to arrange for someone to meet me in Turangi for a refuel.

Lew flew down to catch my final night in Wellington and decided to ride home with me in the new car. I seem to recall a couple of the musos coming along for the drive too. Anyway, Lew settled down in the back and immediately nodded off. A couple of hours into the trip the weather turned against us. We were soon pushing through torrential rain and before long the road was completely awash. I have to mention here that Lew had a thing about his hair; it was never out of place. In the middle of summer he would drive around with the windows up, so as not to mess up his coiffed golden thatch. As there was no air-conditioning back then we used to just about suffocate for the sake of his hair. Hmmmm. . . . The road, in parts, had completely washed away and the rain was ceaseless. Lew was snoring away in the back with his head against the Monaro's very small rear-side window. As this window was tiny, electric, and most important I had the controls, it could be dropped and raised in a flash. All I needed was the perfect puddle and a little careful timing. I launched the car at the centre of a small lake on the road and hit the window switch. As we roared through the water, the window dropped, spray from the front wheel formed a wave that crashed in through the open rear window towards Lew's still sleeping head and slosh — he was soaked! I hit the button again and the window shot up. Unfortunately his very wet (and rather untidy) hair got caught in the window as it closed. That's gotta hurt! What a shocker of a way to wake up. There he was, poor Lew, dangling from the closed window by his hair, soaked to the skin. I had to pull over as we were all laughing so hard and the car windows were totally fogged over. Lew wouldn't talk to me for the rest of that trip, but what amazes me is that he never seemed to learn. He rode with me to Rotorua where the band and I were doing a cabaret show with Larry Morris and his band. Larry and I decided to throw away the prepared format and combine our two bands and just have fun, something Lew was dead against. He never liked me to change my show, but we did it and had a ball.

The next morning before heading back to Auckland we went out to Te Kuiti, to visit Darryl Sampbell. He was an old friend and we knew him from the days when he managed John Farnham. He had a racehorse out there on a property and we had said we'd come by to see it. So, with Lew still carrying on and on about how it was important not to deviate from the programme of the show, blah blah blah, we headed out for Auckland via Te Kuiti. I was driving a black Jaguar XJ6 at the time, very fast and very comfortable. Lew kept on and on and on at me about the show, and the more he went on the faster I drove, hoping to shut him up. We hurtled around a bend (we had driven on this part of the road the day before on the way down) and ran out of road. The Ministry of Works' boys had dug it up and all that was left were huge piles of gravel. I have no idea how fast we were travelling at the time, but I did manage to keep control. I 'controlled' the car straight into a mountain of gravel. After a tremendous rumble, my Jag was buried in a combination of sand and sharp little pebbles, three-quarters of the way up the bonnet. When the dust finally settled, through the filth on the window I could just make out

Right: Lew, me and Bob Hope, backstage at the Auckland Town Hall, 'Bob Hope Show', late 1970s. I opened for him.

ROB GUEST COLLECTION

Left: Me, Bob and my bow tie.

ROB GUEST COLLECTION

a bunch of blokes leaning on their shovels as they laughed their heads off. Lew was screaming, 'You tried to kill me!', and I'm sure he actually believed it. A Maori guy ambled over and drawled, 'You're stuck.' Well, I could have told him that. In the end Lew had to walk to the local pub and buy a slab of beer for the boys, to convince them to help dig and drag us out, which took hours. All the time the boys laughed and said that they never would have thought they'd see me digging roads. Ain't life strange . . .

As a motoring fanatic, I have owned some 70 cars in my time — yes, 70! I began with a MKII Zephyr that I bought from my Dad for $500 and it just grew from there. My fascination for fast cars has never waned and even though I have owned just about every type built, I still get a kick out of seeing one that is in great nick and well loved, no matter what it is. I take my children, and often their friends, to the motor show each year and we all love ogling the latest and greatest autos.

Some cars have not been kind to me though, such as my 1972 MGBT that used to pressurise its petrol tank and just stop, usually in the middle of peak-hour traffic. There was also a bright orange Mercedes 450 SL that I had out on a test drive, when it conked out in front of Westlake Girls' High School, at home-time . . . not funny. The worst car I ever owned was a Triumph Stag — it could overheat in Antarctica. My father was forever buying lottery tickets and while I owned that car, the syndicate name was 'Goodbye Stag' because he saw it was costing me so much! Someone told me once, much too late to help, that if you toss the original motor out and put in a Leyland P76 motor it becomes a great car. Oh well. So, if that was the worst car I'd ever owned, what was my favourite, I hear you ask? To be fair, my list spans decades, and to compare a 1960s car to any of my recent models would be a little unfair. It's enough to say that, having owned everything from Ferraris to Holden panel vans, Triumphs to BMWs, I have a good understanding of the range and I enjoy constantly learning about them all. These days, I don't exchange my cars so quickly; I tend to keep them for at least a couple of years, instead of a couple of weeks.

Being on the road as much as I was meant that I was away from home for weeks, even months, at a time. Lynette was flat out with her career and we seemed like ships passing in the night. The inevitable happened and we split up, with Lynette heading to London — not because of the break-up, but to check out work prospects.

By 1979 I was lucky enough to have won most of the major music awards, I had toured the country from one end to the other numerous times, and while I had no desire to leave what had well and truly become my home country, I felt that I had exhausted the circuit in New Zealand. I applied for a grant from the New Zealand Arts Council to travel, and study theatre overseas. I received a $2000 grant, which I put towards airfares. Lew and I took off for the West End, Broadway and Las Vegas for six weeks, to broaden our outlook. We took in many shows and I quickly realised that it doesn't matter where you perform, as long as when you perform it's to the best of your ability. I mean, a thousand people in the audience in a London theatre is the same as a thousand people in Timaru — no matter who or where they are, they deserve the best show possible.

While in London, we went to see Bob Hope at the Palladium. I had supported Bob in Auckland earlier that year and he had given us an open invitation to visit him in London. Not really one for taking up these sorts of invitations, it took a lot to convince me to take that visit backstage. I never go backstage after anyone else's show, I just don't feel comfortable. Having been coerced into going to the dressing rooms, we met Bob and he was wonderful. I recall he had been so in Auckland too, even coming to my dressing room to compliment me on the show. Mike Harvey (who was musical director for me in that show) and I both felt inspired by this legendary gentleman and both of us appreciated his warmth. So, there we were, backstage at the London Palladium, being served drinks by Bob Hope's assistant, when the door flew open and in bounced Tommy Cooper (minus the fez) straight out of my childhood. He threw his arms around Bob, said a cheery hello to us, and although he really had no idea who we were, he chimed, 'Anybody got a camera?' in just the same fashion we'd all heard him deliver his catchphrase, 'Not like that . . . like THAT!' Well, I was bowled over. I grew up watching him on television and as a kid I'd imitated him as everyone else had. This was a very clever man and to have him standing there, right in front of me, beside Bob Hope, was too much to bear. We all burst out laughing and spent much of that evening exchanging crazy stories. Since then, of course, Tommy Cooper has sadly passed away.

I had to keep quiet about the fact that I had a 35 mm camera, complete with flash and fresh batteries, in my bag by the couch, but I couldn't shake the feeling that it may have been a little tacky to start taking photos in this very private arena. When I finally told Lew, much later of course, he was not a happy chap. What manager would be happy about missing an opportunity like that? Now, though, as there is a photo missing from my story, I am beginning to think he may have been right.

It might appear, from the way I speak of Lew, that our relationship was anything but friendly. This is far from the truth — Lew and I were a team for almost 19 years, and in this time we shared our successes and failures. We agreed on matters one moment and disagreed on others the next, but in the final analysis I know that no one was more dedicated to making a success of my career than Lew. He was a very dear friend. Shortly before my career began to take off in Australia, Lew died. I still feel somehow bereft of his counsel, but his sound advice and 'golden rules' have become part of me, and I think — and hope — he is smiling now.

We travelled from London to New York and saw many fine shows on Broadway. We also managed to catch up with David Livingstone, the writer of the American song from the Pacific Song Contest. David showed us around Manhattan and we ended up at a club called Jo Allen's (a hangout for the stars). Everyone who was anyone had their photo, larger than life, on the wall at Jo Allen's. It was here that I was introduced to Moosehead beer. This drop, I was to discover, has a kick more like the other end of the beast. We had been laughing and talking for hours, when Lew said, 'Rob, sitting at the table behind you is Burt Bacharach.' Well in my, let's say very relaxed state, I stood up and virtually yelled, 'Burt Bacharach! Where?' The room went silent. Burt, who had his back to me, turned around, smiled and said quietly, 'Hi.' It was one of those moments when you wish the ground would just open up and swallow you. So, as the place bubbled up with laughter, I sat down and made myself a mental note to have the volume switch on my voice-box checked. Lew stormed out in embarrassment and headed back to the hotel, leaving David and me to party on. By morning Lew had settled down but I could tell he was definitely not amused. Funny that, Burt has never written a song for me either. Hmm . . .

Meatloaf was at the number one chart spot everywhere at this time, and we lined up a meeting with his management. We wanted to talk about United States representation and the possibility of making a clip in New York for my recording of 'Winter in America' from my album *Dedication*. We met in a suite on the top floor of a building in New York that seemed to tower above the other skyscrapers. Behind a huge desk was The Manager. He seemed interested in our proposal and agreed to represent us. All he said he needed was a retainer fee with no guarantees. WHAT?

Opposite page: A publicity shot, believe it or not, for *Playboy*, Chicago. It's a hard life . . .

We talked about the film clip and off the top of his head he nominated the figure $US30,000. This was for ONE song, back in 1978. You could have bought a house for that back home then, and had money left over for a new car and a holiday. Needless to say we declined this kind offer and my United States debut was put off for a few years.

Our Arts Grant odyssey had also taken us to Toronto, where I performed on the 'Bob McLean Television Show', and to Chicago, where we stayed at the Playboy Club. I even had my photo taken with the Bunnies. The shot appeared in an issue of the magazine a couple of months later. Not many guys can say they posed for *Playboy* — or want to, I suppose — but everything was very proper and we had lots of good clean fun.

By the time we arrived in Las Vegas we were tired, to say the least, but now was no time to slow down. Every entertainer we admired was in town doing one show or another. Tina Turner was sharing the bill with Lou Rawls . . . yep, on the SAME show. Dean Martin was on and so were Andy Williams, Tom Jones and Wayne Newton. All of these stars could be seen for a three-drink minimum, though in most places the drinks were free. In those days, hotels charged around $15 a night and entry to the live shows was cheap. This was showbiz Mecca and the two of us, who both love shows, caught an average of two each night while we were there. I was on a health kick at the time and at 5.30 one morning I decided to pull on the old tracksuit and head out for a jog. Past the hotel reception I went, stretching and preparing. I stepped from the air-conditioned lobby into the early morning HEAT . . . wow! 116 degrees at 6.30 a.m! So as not to look stupid, I began to run. By the time I'd reached the corner of the strip where Caesar's Palace, The Dunes, MGM and Flamingo all meet, I was dripping wet. I looked like I'd just climbed out of the pool, and as I stood there melting in the heat, a hooker ambled over and tried to pick me up. She HAD to be joking. I turned around and slithered back to the hotel, trying not to look conspicuous (yeah, right), and never tried that again. Lew and I spent a few days resting in Honolulu before the long flight home.

After returning to New Zealand I continued my theatre contracts. While I was in Dunedin rehearsing for a season of *Half a Sixpence*, I received a call at my hotel one sunny Friday morning (funny how those details remain etched in your mind). My father had passed away. Mum told me he had been chatting to her while sitting in the car, stopped at a set of traffic lights on the way to work, when he suffered an aneurysm. He just went. That sunny morning took on a surreal quality and I became numb. All I could think about was getting home. All the flights were full, I had an opening night a week away, but I had to get home. I raced out to Dunedin airport and waited for a cancellation — nothing. Someone finally told me there was a vacancy on a flight to Christchurch, so I grabbed it, then had to wait three more painful hours at Christchurch airport before a seat became available to Auckland. A whole day had passed before I reached home and I was frantic. My family had always been close, so my world felt as though it were crumbling when I lost Dad. As much as I know there is a world out there full of people who have lost loved ones, I'm sure you'll understand when I say I felt alone in my agony. I needed desperately to be there for my mother and Dave, so we could all help each other.

My last memory of Dad was of the day he drove me to the airport in my car. I was off to Dunedin and he, with a cheeky grin on his face said, 'Don't worry Son, I'll look after it for you!' Then he took off, my Dad at the wheel of a sports car. He was delighted and he looked fantastic! As it turned out, he was driving my car that fateful Friday. I thank God that it had not happened a few minutes

MELBOURNE SUNDAY HERALD SUPPLEMENT, 3 DECEMBER 1989

SUNDAY HERALD

DECEMBER 3, 1989

AT LAST! LES MISERABLES HITS MELBOURNE

Front page of the *Sunday Herald* supplement. John Diedrich as Javert; me seated as Jean Valjean.

Isn't he beautiful . . . my boy, Christopher.

Right: Family outing. Jude, Chris and friend.

Below: Amy at seven years old, and flowers, Perth 1998. Taken for a fashion layout for *Destinations* magazine.

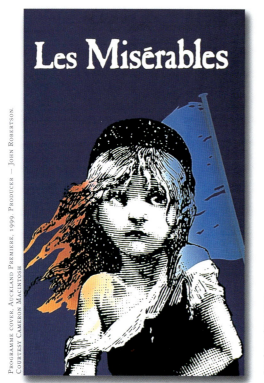

FROM *LES MISÉRABLES* PROGRAMME — 10TH ANNIVERSARY PRODUCTION; PRODUCER — JOHN ROBERTSON; PHOTOGRAPHY — MICHAEL LE POER TRENCH AND ROBERT MCFARLANE. COURTESY CAMERON MACINTOSH

Top left: The famous *Les Miserables* image.

Top right: Waiting in the wings for an entrance in *Les Miserables*, as the mayor.

Left: The make-up process is serious business — ageing Jean Valjean, in the second act.

Above: One of my favourite scenes from *Les Miserables* — end of Act II.

Right: As Jean Valjean — before climbing over the barricade.

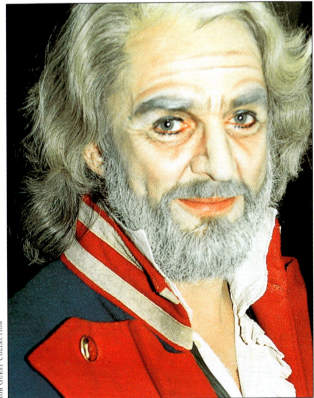

ROB GUEST COLLECTION

Right: Convict Valjean 24601. Return season, 10th Anniversary Tour — Auckland, 1999.

Below: Backstage with my understudy Rowan — that's me on the left.

From left: me, my assistant Norman Goodwin, Peter Cousens, Philip Quast and William Zappa.

Top: 'The Boys' Club' — on our first outing.
Bottom: I catch a Banjo shark . . . now what? Adelaide.

With Tina Cross at The Ace of Clubs, Auckland.

earlier, as he and Mum were negotiating peak-hour traffic across the Auckland Harbour Bridge. Dave and I helped Mum organise the funeral, and by the following Tuesday I had Mum with me on my way back to Dunedin. Getting her away seemed the right thing for her at the time. My father was, and still is, the BEST Dad ever. He was always there for us when we needed him as we grew up. He used to love coming to all my shows, even those of my school-days. He and Mum encouraged me to follow my dream and I will always cherish their support. For Dad, as much as anything else, I will always pursue my dream. Dad had a good voice and my early years were filled with the music of Paul Robson or Al Jolson, always sung by Dad 'in character'. He was even cast in a play shortly before he died. Of course we all went to see him perform. I remember waiting the whole play through just to hear his one line (delivered superbly) and then see him unceremoniously dumped in a trash bin and dragged off stage. Talk about a laugh, it was hilarious. Each and every show I do, I dedicate to 'John Guest', and I feel his presence every step of the way. At the end of the Dunedin season we moved back to Auckland. I miss you Dad.

Every time I ventured overseas, I found it very hard to settle down on my return. The trip to the United States had stirred in me a need to travel and perform and it took a long time for me to get back into the swing of things. Then, fortune smiled on me again. Lew called to let me know Howard

Morrison was putting together a show for the New Zealand Tourism Board. This show, called 'Come On to New Zealand', was designed as a whistle-stop promotional tour of the United States. The organisers wanted me to come along and participate in a couple of medleys and perform one solo song, a Tony Baker composition, 'I Know a Country'. We were booked to play one-night stands only and the plan was to completely circumnavigate North America and Canada in six extremely busy weeks. We put the show together in New Zealand, and right up to the day before we left we were learning and rehearsing from early in the morning, 'til late into the night. I was even practising in the car on my way in. At 8 o'clock in the morning, just two days before we were due to leave for the States, I was singing away in my much-loved black Jag, on my way across the Auckland Harbour Bridge, when all hell broke loose. Three lanes of traffic tangled in a smash and I was right in the middle. I swung the steering wheel in an attempt to get the heck out of there, and while I didn't get loose I did manage to dodge all but a truck, which connected with my Jag's front left quarter. Amazingly my car was still drivable; I was a lot better off than nearly all the 11 other cars involved. When the jam finally cleared, hours later, I was able to drive to rehearsal. I launched into one of the numbers and everything started to spin. I must have hit my head in the accident. 'This is not good,' they declared, and rushed me to a specialist. Sure enough, the doctors found I had concussion and ordered me not to fly for at least 48 hours . . . sure! Luckily, I managed to convince a doctor to give me a further check-up the next day, and I was able to fly out to Honolulu on schedule.

We were to be a travelling advertisement for New Zealand, primarily for American travel agents who apparently thought New Zealand too out of the way to include as a tourist destination, but actually had not the foggiest idea where or who we were. So our performance was preceded by a documentary film, with New Zealand in all its glory — magnificent countryside, warm smiles and a cultural note or two. We were indeed proud Kiwis, ambassadors for the Land of the Long White Cloud. This was a whirlwind. We would arrive at a new city each morning, early, have a sound-check at the venue, grab something to eat, put on the show, then head back to whichever hotel we were to stay at and crash. We even performed on the 'Dinah Shore Show' in Los Angeles, and here we really found out how little Yanks knew about New Zealand culture. So, we were to sell, sell, sell — or should I say, educate, educate, educate. We had to haka in Hawaii and aroha in Alabama. We performed in nightclubs in New York and fair grounds in Arizona — you name it, we did it. On Saint Patrick's Day we found ourselves in Chicago, where, in typical American fashion, they'd dyed the river green and most of the beer in town (we were told) was served green. We performed in the bitterly cold outdoors, as part of the celebrations, though I'm still not sure how 'Hoki Mai' fitted the theme. One night in Los Angeles, Tina Cross decided to call Lynette, who was performing at The Dunes Hotel in Vegas. I spoke with her and made plans to fly up. She organised a meeting with Frederic Apcar, a very well-known producer, who set up an audition for me. I sang, and later that day was offered a place in the long-running *Casino de Paris*.

I guess I had really begun to understand that being an entertainer meant travelling to where the work was. It would have been too easy to settle within my comfort zone in New Zealand, but the idea of just doing the odd 'special', singing the occasional jingle and enjoying theatrical seasons as interesting roles came up was just never going to be enough for me. I always need a challenge. Some have said I'm a workaholic, but I don't see it that way. How lucky I am to have a deep, abiding passion . . . it seems a rare thing these days. To be able to make a living doing what I am addicted to is just the most amazing bonus. It is almost impossible to explain. On stage, as I have mentioned before, is where I feel most comfortable. I wish for everyone the same joy, but I'm glad you don't all want to be on the stage!

I flew back to New Zealand because I had a contract to perform in *Jesus Christ Superstar* in Rotorua. I also did a television special for TV1 and Canadian Broadcasting called 'Kaye and Guest' with Gloria Kaye, the Canadian singer from the Pacific Song Contest. We shot footage around the Coromandel, and ended the show with a concert in the studio at Avalon, Wellington. The show was aired in New Zealand a couple of times and I believe (strange as it may seem) Turkish television picked it up.

Lynette flew back to New Zealand and we were married before returning to take up residency in Vegas. *Casino de Paris* had been running for 18 years and was something of an icon among icons on the strip. Beautiful costumes, stunning sets, gorgeous showgirls and dancers, exotic animals; you name it, it had a spot in the show. I joined the show on an H2 visa, which enabled me to sing anddance but nothing else. I couldn't even pump gas. This visa was tight and the time-limit was so strict, I remember being flown to Calgary, Canada, one morning and having to grab a cab to the United States Consulate to get my passport stamped to prove I had left the United States. Then I had to catch a plane back to Vegas in time for the show. Quite bizarre — leaving a country to get a visa so I could stay.

Jon Lexia was the orchestra maestro — a very volatile and pedantic but brilliant Frenchman. I rehearsed my own segment of the show with Jon, and his orchestra was magnificent. I was in heaven. Vegas! We performed two shows a night and had one night off each week. That amounts to a heck of a lot of singing, and in the very hot, dry and dusty conditions of Vegas, I quickly learned the local phrase, 'Vegas Throat'. This is a condition brought about by desiccating air-conditioning. Las Vegas, Nevada, is a glittering oasis in a large inhospitable desert. A number of headliners, such as Tom Jones, make a habit of arriving well before their booked dates to get acclimatised; even Elvis used to do it. So, like athletes, we went into training for the show. I knew we had to, because there is always that queue of artists as I mentioned earlier, ready to take over from you if you're not up to it. I drank gallons of water to stave off dehydration and managed to hang on to my voice.

We bought a house, with a pool, just behind The Sahara. I spent countless nights sleeping on an airbed in the pool as the heat was unbearable, even in the air-conditioned house. It's not a pleasant wake-up call, however, when you roll over in the night. I saw so many great acts during my time in Vegas that after a while I guess I became a little blasé. Friends would come to town and ask me who was playing and where, and I would have to confess to them that I had no idea. I never tired of the bright lights and festival atmosphere but I no longer had to drive The Strip so as not to miss anything any more. I just got on with business. It suited me to use the freeway, instead of The Strip, to travel to and from The Dunes — it offered me time to think and clear my head.

Every Wednesday night our orchestra had a night off, and the swing band would step in. These guys were hired to take over from every orchestra on The Strip on their night off. So, on a Tuesday they played Caesar's Palace, where they may have supported Diana Ross, and on Thursday they were at The MGM with Barry Manilow or Frank Sinatra or Sammy Davis Jnr. This band was hot, and I loved Wednesdays.

I became very friendly with the magic troupe at The Dunes. They were known as The Fercos and their act involved tigers, leopards and a beautiful lion called Caesar. This magnificent beast was the son of Elsa, the lioness from the movie *Born Free*, and a more majestic creature you will never see. To look at him made me feel deep, sincere respect. This was 900kgs of pure king of the jungle. The head of the family clan, Ferco himself, said, 'Rob, why don't you have your photo taken with Caesar?' 'Yeah, right,' I thought, 'me and a lion! Sure, I can't wait.' But Ferco was tenacious and one night I finally said OK. The handlers put Caesar on top of a remodelled golf cart, which, from the audience, looked like a huge shimmering star. I clambered aboard and took my spot next to this leviathan only to realise with a start that no one was holding him. Regaining my balance, I searched the room for some security, preferably a guard, with a gun. No one, not a soul. Oh, my God!

Ferco — from a long distance away, I might add — said, 'Rob, show no fear!' You have got to be kidding. My knees were knocking as I mouthed, 'Take the damn photo! Quick!'

Ferco, still from the rear of the room then offered, 'Get closer to Caesar.'

Well, I moved closer but declared to myself I was going to kill one magician, if I managed to get out of this predicament alive. Ferco piped up yet again and said, 'Put your arm around Caesar.'

Facing my fear head on, I reached out, slowly, to touch Caesar, again while I pleaded, 'Take the bloody photo!'

Again, Ferco (the walking dead man) said, 'Get CLOSER, Rob!'

I inched a little closer until finally Ferco declared the setting ready. Just then, Caesar turned his mighty head toward me and let out an enormous, ferocious sounding, roar. OH MY GOD!!

Ferco very unkindly burst into laughter at my pallor. It made for a great photo but I have to say I have no idea how I got down from the cart, or to my dressing room; it's all a blur. Thinking about that moment still makes my legs turn to jelly — I must have been mad.

The Dunes show was full of variety, never a dull moment as they say. Along with magic acts, singers, exotic animals and comedians, I had the chance to work with some wonderful specialty acts. The Nicolodese were a specialty tumbling, balancing act of amazing talent. They would masterfully climb a flight of stairs in a one-handed handstand, then flip into a tumbling sequence and land with dazzling precision. I usually watched their antics from the wings but on one occasion stayed in my dressing room during their act. The Fercos finished their last illusion and began to make their way off stage. Sheba the cheetah was, as usual, on top of the 'star' cart and Caesar was sitting to one side. Tony Ferco, in his usual way, joked with the audience, 'Sheba jump, I miss, you catch!' which brought its usual huge laugh.

Now, what usually happened was that Sheba would leap from the star, in the direction of the audience but Ferco would grab her lead rope and steer her in the direction of the wings. On this occasion the Nicolodese's mother was watching from my regular spot in the wings. She was standing behind a curtain when Sheba sensed her presence and leapt.

No one really knew what was going on when the stage manager signalled me to the stage. The audience, it seemed, had heard the commotion but were not aware of what had actually happened. I cued the orchestra and away we went. When I left the stage I finally found out that Sheba had taken a large piece from Mrs Nicolodese's calf and they had rushed her to hospital. The poor woman would never make the mistake of hanging around that show again.

By the time I got back to my dressing room that evening the all-white suit I was wearing and my white shoes were spattered with blood. I still don't know whether the audience saw it, but my dresser sure did — man, was he cranky. Still, he eventually managed to get it all clean, only to have the Wardrobe Master declare it was not glitzy enough for Vegas anyway and whisk it away. I had worn this suit in the Pacific Song Contest and it held a special place in my collection but I bravely let it go.

When the suit came back to me, just two days later, it was amazing. The wardrobe wizards had sewn tiny mirrors all over the jacket, in patterns. That night I wore it on stage and became a human mirror ball. I reckon that's where they got the idea for Robert Redford's *The Electric*

Horseman. Talk about blinding your audience . . . it was incredible.

The Dunes was a rabbit warren backstage, with tunnels enabling acts to get to and from the stage without having to go through the casino. I used to enter one of these tunnels from the car park each evening. This tunnel had only three doorways — mine from the car park in the middle, the stage exit at one end and the loading dock at the other. One night I was coming in from the car park and turning down the tunnel to the stage only to find Caesar's cage blocking my way. When I turned to find another way around, I realised that the animal handlers were oblivious to my presence, pushing a cage full of Bengal tigers down the tunnel toward me. These were large cages that the Fercos used to cart the animals to and from the casino complex each evening. There was no going over them, as they were about a foot below the ceiling in height, and no room under or around them — I was trapped. The Fercos were short-handed that night, so they were all running, madly trying to keep things moving smoothly. When I looked up, I realised that in their rush they had put Sheba the cheetah on top of the second cage, believing no one was around. She had spotted me and was now ready to pounce. My blood ran cold. I called out to Ferco who said, 'Don't move a muscle.' This guy was just full of great ideas. He had to be joking, not one muscle in my body was standing still! Suddenly the door to the stage opened and Caesar's cage was dragged through — I was free. I shook for a solid half-hour and insisted thereafter that the middle door down the corridor remain locked while the animals were being shifted. This business can be hazardous to your health!

The union demands that were eventually placed on the producers of this extravaganza *Casino de Paris* became impossible and the owners finally opted for a change. They turned The Dunes into a 'Star Room', where the focus of the evening was on single performers; I believe Robert Goulet took up residence for a while afterward.

The next stop for me turned out to be across the United States, in Atlantic City. Frederic Apcar was producing a show called *Stepping Out* in the main room at Harrah's Hotel. He was unhappy with the singer and offered me the contract. Believe it or not, this took some serious consideration. I would have to step into an awkward situation, where the current singer had made friends and moulded the arrangements to suit his style. Nevertheless, I took the job, learned the dance sequences and songs within a week, and was on that stage before my feet had really touched the ground. The hotel was full when I arrived, and as I knew the show was to run for three months I needed to find an apartment. To give myself some time to look properly, I booked into a local motel.

The rather dingy motel seemed inordinately quiet. Still, by the time I'd finished my incredibly long first day's work I was too weary to care. It didn't even bother me, much, that the only light burning in the whole motel was the one over the door to my room on the second floor. I turned a dark corner and began to climb the stairs when I noticed a black dog asleep on a rubbish bin. Not one to just wander up to strays, I kept my distance. When it saw me and leapt up I realised how wise I had been — this was not a dog but the most enormous rat I had ever seen. I don't know who jumped the highest, me or the rat, but luckily it took off. I scurried to my room and spent the rest of the night listening to scratching and clawing and cringed at the occasional squeals coming from behind the walls. There was a plate on the wall beside the bed, and periodically it would bang loudly as the rodent tore away at the wall behind it. It was an appalling night. It seemed each time I managed to convince myself to ignore the squeals and nod off, the bang of the plate would wake me with a start. Having had next to no sleep at all, I staggered to the reception desk in the morning to tell them of my plight. Their response was, 'What do you expect, Mister? You are our only guest. The place is condemned and it will be pulled down any day now.' Obviously I had to get out of there — fast. For the remainder of my Atlantic City stay, I lived on the island of Brigantine. It was really close to work and I was able to share digs with a fellow cast member.

I had rented a bomb from a company called Just 4 Wheels and that was exactly what it had. It was a load of rubbish, but it was cheap transport. One morning I woke to discover that the whole island was under water. Luckily we were on the second floor. Lucky for us, that is, but not for the car rental company as their old bomb was almost totally submerged, with only its roof visible.

We couldn't leave the house, of course. What a shame — a day of forced rest! When I finally could ring Just 4 Wheels, I had to tell them we couldn't drive their car because it was 'flooded' (ha-ha). They were really good about it and quickly replaced the car for us.

While in Atlantic City I had yet another animal experience — they seem to follow me. I had been to see a show at another casino and arranged to grab a meal later with the comic star of the show. He worked with a troupe of chimpanzees, beautiful little characters, and had put them into his dressing room, given them their supper and a drink and kissed them all goodbye. We left them for about an hour, and when we returned we found that the oldest chimp, being the leader, had unscrewed every light bulb from around the make-up mirror and stacked them perfectly on the floor.

Next stop, Reno, Nevada. Once again I was at a Harrah's Hotel and once again I was to work with Frederic Apcar, this time on a show called *Heat's On*. At this time Lynette was performing in a show in Tahoe as lead dancer. They wanted me to host the show, do a couple of 'production numbers' and a spot in the middle of the programme. I had lots of involvement and a great line-up to work with. I chose to live in Lake Tahoe up in the hills over Reno. Tahoe was beautiful with hot, sunny summers and freezing, snowy winters. Reno, on the other hand, was a cowboy town. So, I used to drive down the mountain to Reno each afternoon to work and happily back up again after the final show each night. I could go boating during the day and perform each night, and used to play racquet ball with Sammy Davis Jnr's nephew, who was working as Sammy's sound-man. I was a happy man and I thoroughly enjoyed my stay in Lake Tahoe.

Heat's On shared a choreographer, the very clever Ronnie Lewis, with none other than Liza Minnelli. Sammy Davis Jnr was a huge fan of Ronnie's work so we used to see them at our shows from time to time. The fact is there was a constant stream of icons to be spotted in the audience — singers such as John Denver and a variety of celebrities and notable personalities. It never ceased to amaze me. The band, headed by drummer Jon Melia, was seated behind a plexiglass screen on the mezzanine floor, above the audience. On any night I might look up there to see people 'sitting in'. One night a member of the Doobie Brothers was in to catch the show — apparently he was a friend of one of the guys in the band. This night, just before I went on stage, I was told that both Sammy and Liza were in. Did that put the pressure on? You betcha! Once we'd finished the show however, several bottles of Dom Perignon arrived backstage with compliments from Sammy. It seemed he loved the show. He also sent the cast an invitation to his penthouse suite. When we arrived, his assistant, George, ushered us through to a sumptuous suite where Sammy was waiting to greet us. We were captivated and barely noticed the only other person in the room, who was curled up on a sofa in track pants and fluffy slippers. After a few moments of conversation, Sammy asked me if I had met Liza — yep, it was Liza on the sofa. What an evening! We all had a great time swapping stories and Sammy gave me some valuable advice. At that time I was singing current songs, Lionel Ritchie covers etc., but he suggested what was missing was a standard, a song everyone knows. I took his advice and from the very next rehearsal I incorporated one long-standing popular song. It worked a treat and Sammy did sneak in one night to see if I'd followed his tip. I believe he was pleased that I'd listened. It's not every day that you're offered advice from a master. I took the opportunity, when I could, to see his show and I learned so very much from him. It's amazing how much you learn by just watching and listening, and not just to the stars either. I find there are so many lessons to be learned from all sorts of performers and productions, and sometimes it's just as important to see what NOT to do.

One balmy afternoon when I entered the casino in Reno I noticed a guy playing blackjack. That was hardly unusual as it's a very popular game, but this guy was on his own, playing two or three hands at once and doing very well. When the first of the evening shows was over, I came out to find he was still there, but this time he was surrounded by a crowd and had amassed quite a pile of chips. I did the next show and was heading home through the casino when I realised he was still at it, now with a huge pile of chips and flanked by security guards. I left the happy gambler and went home to Tahoe. Incredibly, he was still there when I arrived the next day, fenced in by coffee cups, empty food plates and the ever-growing pile of chips — not the edible kind. Two shows later, as I headed back through the casino for home, I realised he was gone. I asked the 'pit' boss what had happened to the 'blackjack king'. He told me that the guy had set himself a target of a quarter of a million dollars, and had reached $230,000 when he started to lose. He chased his losses and in no time at all had lost the lot. The boss told me the fellow was in the coffee shop and the hotel were picking up the bill to his room and his meal. My lesson here, obviously, was that all those beautiful hotels and casinos are not built by the winners, but by the losers.

I had gambled when I first hit Las Vegas. I remember one night a bunch of us hit The Flamingo. It's very dangerous in those places, as you can go to the cashier's cage and cash your pay cheque very easily, making it, sadly, too easy to give your money back to the people you have earned it from. On this particular night I too was playing blackjack, otherwise known as pontoon, or simply 21. It doesn't take too long to get the hang of it, and pretty quickly you're no longer embarrassing yourself by placing 'mug' bets or splitting a perfectly good pair of 10s or 'hitting' 18s etc. We were all having a great time and I was playing and winning well, until around 5 a.m., when my luck took a serious U-turn — I could not win a hand. I tried betting less, then betting more, missing a hand, nothing worked. By 8 a.m. I was down to my last $10 note. I took a break and went to the bathroom, where a glance in the mirror revealed more than I expected. I hardly recognised my reflection — my eyes were blood red, my skin was grey and I generally looked terrible. I had lost a week's pay . . . what a clown. 'If only I could win some of it back,' I thought aloud, then immediately wondered how many times that had been uttered, even prayed, in this tiled room. I splashed my face with cold water and headed back to the table where the dealer had changed. I placed my $10 on the table and was dealt my cards. First a Queen, then an Ace — blackjack, paying $15. So then I had $25. I let it ride and won again — even money this time, so then I had $50. This went on for the next hour and I managed to win back almost all of my money. I couldn't believe it. Never again would I gamble my hard-earned money. On that day I set myself a strict rule: I would take out maybe $50 and when it was gone that would be the end of my gambling for the night. If I happened to win anything, I would pocket my own money and play only with the casino's. After all, the money you win isn't yours until you manage to walk out the door with it.

There are far too many ways to lose it again while you're within their walls.

That same morning, at another table, there was another singer from our group who was also having a bad time. He asked me for a loan and against my better judgement I gave him $100. He put it down and won, and doubled it on the next hand. I grabbed his arm at this point, took back my $100 and took him to breakfast. Gambling can be so addictive if you let it, especially when you live in America's gambling playgrounds like Las Vegas. I have seen people lose everything, absolutely everything, and believe me there are many more stories of losses than successes in this area. The losses can drive people crazy, normal people can be pushed to outrageous lengths when they become desperate. The secret is to know how much you are willing to lose. If you win, it's a bonus — walk away.

Heat's On tranferred to Lake Tahoe at Harrahs. Halfway through a show one night, pandemonium broke out in the casino. People started falling into the showroom yelling and screaming. I continued to sing even though I could see, through the open door in the back of the room, people lying on the floor and a security guard leaning on a blackjack table with his gun drawn. Things were not orderly this evening. My song finished, everyone was still yelling and screaming. The band had no idea what was going on as they could not see anything from the mezzanine. Now, I could have just left the stage, and it probably would have been the smart thing to do. I didn't because I knew that the next scheduled number involved a lot of people coming onto the stage and the situation looked perilous so I cued the band to play a different song.

By the time I'd finished, the drama was over and people had begun to settle down. Once backstage I found out that apparently someone had tried to hold up the cashier's cage. He had fired a gun and the bullet had passed right through two walls before lodging itself in a cubicle wall in the ladies' bathroom, inches from where some poor lady was minding her business. An off-duty security guard had wrestled the would-be robber to the ground and there was a SWAT team on a roof over the road, waiting for his exit. Unbelievable, frightening stuff. As I listened to these explanations it suddenly occurred to me how ridiculous I had been. I mean to say, I had no idea what was going on, what if the gunman had decided he didn't like my choice of song? I'd have been a sitting duck. There I had been, on stage, in a spotlight, in front of a gunman. Oh no . . . I feel one of those shaky moments coming on, again.

Mother Nature eventually forced the show in Tahoe to close. Our audience was always primarily made up of tourists or skiers or holiday-makers in general and that season, in terms of snowfall, was pitiful. Lake Tahoe, the primary resort area these folks came to stay in, straddles the states of Nevada and California, with one road out to Reno and one road out to Sacramento. When the heavy dump of fresh snow finally came, very late into the season, it caused the road to collapse. As a result, we were stranded, isolated from any tourist traffic for a few days. This hurt all the local businesses but, as was necessary, the first thing to close was the show.

As one door closes, so they say . . . Television New Zealand called. They wanted me to take part in the opening of the Michael Fowler Centre in Wellington. It's almost as though they had a crystal ball, as their calls usually came with perfect timing. So after three and a half years in the States I returned to good old New Zealand. With mixed emotions I landed in Auckland. It was great to be home, but my departure had not been easy and it was coming back to haunt me. So, when I arrived back in New Zealand, I was a little uneasy. Mum was the one who had convinced me to go in the first place, to keep to my promise of following the dream. It was all the memories of Dad and the sad, sad moments of parting that rushed back at me when I got home that I had a hard time with. Mum was doing pretty well. I had, of course, kept in close touch with her the whole time I was away. She had bought her own house and had begun to rebuild her life. I settled down. At least, I attempted to!

Maybe they're right, those people who say going home and slipping back into an old routine is hard. We do have a more relaxed and less stressed way of life when we're surrounded by family and friends, the treadmill does move more slowly. It is just that it's such a difficult gear change to make, if you've been travelling and at a frantic pace. Still, I had been lured home by the promise of work, and work I did — until it basically ran out. I was then at somewhat of a loose end. What was I going to do next? I had been working consistently for a long time by then, and along with that came a regular income. That had also stopped, of course, so I distracted myself with a hobby for a while.

I had purchased a beautiful Z28 Chevrolet Camaro while in Lake Tahoe and had driven it to San Francisco with a view to bringing it home to New Zealand. A few conversations with my contacts in the motor industry quickly revealed how expensive and time-consuming this little exercise was going to be. Cars, you may recall, are one of my main passions, so, despite all the warnings, I knew I simply had to have it back in New Zealand. I was doing the odd commercial and television show and that kept things ticking along while I waited what turned out to be six months for my precious cargo. When my lovely car finally arrived, I was baffled by its state. The windscreen and stereo had been replaced and, peculiarly, none of the tyres matched any more. When I had handed it over to the shipping company, all was in order. I can only imagine that it had been broken into while it stood waiting to be transported. Trying to get answers to my myriad questions was unbelievable. Everyone passed the buck.

As the car had not been driven for so long, supposedly sitting in its container, I had asked that a sign, saying 'PLEASE DON'T START' be painted on the windscreen. When I arrived with a car trailer and a mechanic to collect it, there was the sign on the windshield, but the car was out of its container. So I asked the rather obvious question about why the car was now parked in the lot rather than still in its box, and they said they had driven it out. Well, I reckon they'd have just about had to drive with their head out the side window because the sign almost totally obscured the view through the front. I suppose they were either a little slow, or, the chance to drive one of these beauties was just too much of a temptation (I can relate to that!). It was, after all, one of the first of its kind in New Zealand. From that day on this car was, tragically, nothing but trouble. Someone had filled it with leaded fuel — there was no such thing as unleaded in New Zealand at the time. The result was a failure in the catalytic converter, which meant I had to invest $5000 in a gadget that basically lied to the car's on-board computer about the fuel it was working with. What a headache. I could never quite shake the feeling that I wasn't going to get away with this for long, so I made the tough decision to sell and put it in a car yard in Tauranga. It took for ever to sell, and though I would like to believe I broke even on this one, I truly doubt it.

There appeared to be a strange attitude held by some industry people at that time. Some, it seemed, felt I'd been somehow disloyal to the New Zealand market, and although it remained unsaid I'm sure they were thinking, 'I hope you don't think you can just saunter back in where you left off, Buddy.' The tall poppy syndrome was alive and well. On the one hand these self-appointed judges would think, 'Hold on, if he or she is so good, why aren't they busy overseas?' Then once you have stretched your wings and entertained abroad, you come home, feeling loyal to your country and you can hear these same people thinking, 'If he or she is so good, why did they come back?' It is impossible to please all the people, all of the time, so I don't even try. I cooled my heels for a while, recording 'Anthem', a song from a new theatre show called *Chess*, for the World Cup Bowls competition. I worked in the studio with my good pal Carl Doy, who had been my musical director on numerous occasions. Carl was, at the time, about to release 'Piano by Candlelight', a beautiful and very popular album, and I believe he is still New Zealand's biggest-selling recording artist.

Carl asked me, quite out of the blue, to record a composition of his that he wanted to send to the World Song Festival organisers in Los Angeles. To cut a long story short, we were off to Los Angeles. This was to be my third song contest. The first was, of course, the Pacific Song Contest, in which I entered with Mike Harvey and came second. The second, the Korean Song Festival in Seoul, Korea, is one I must tell you more about, later, because it was a most eye-opening experience.

In Los Angeles, we rehearsed with Carl Doy for the World Song Contest in a small downtown studio. The actual performance was to be, as it turned out, in The Shrine, the same theatre in which Michael Jackson's hair was accidentally set alight during the making of a Pepsi commercial. Thankfully, the place was luckier for us. I shared a dressing room with Carl Anderson, who played Judas in the movie *Jesus Christ Superstar,* so there was no shortage of conversation. He is a lovely guy and by the end of the day our managers had concocted the idea that we should do *Superstar* around the United States, where he and I would alternate nightly between playing Jesus and Judas. In case you didn't know, Carl Anderson is an African American and he believed that this would be the first production in which a black man portrayed Jesus. We continued negotiations on our return to New Zealand, but Carl recorded and his song became a hit, so the tour never happened. It is often the case in this industry that even the most detailed plans don't bear fruit. On another occasion, in fact while I was in Las Vegas, I was approached by a producer from Los Angeles to do a movie. It was to be called *Chasing Dreams* and he offered me the lead, alongside Ricardo Montalban, who they hoped would play my manager. We swapped letters of intent, then it all fell through due to funding problems. Who knows where my life may have led, had this opportunity panned out? Perhaps nowhere, but I'll never know, will I? That's showbiz!

5.

Heart and Seoul

ALLOW ME TO TAKE you back to Seoul, Korea, and the Korean Song Festival, where I sang a song by Stephen Bell-Booth, and picked up the Performer's Trophy, along with a swag of new fans. Lew and I spent a couple of weeks in Korea with Stephen and our dear friend Christopher Bourn. I had known Chris for many years through the variety of television shows I'd been involved with, and he was in Korea representing TVNZ. Korea was a bit of a culture shock to all of us. It was the first time I had performed in a country whose first language was not English. We were met at the airport by Mr Kim, a softly-spoken and very polite man, who kindly drove us to the very Western-style Hotel Lotte (later I learned that 'Kim' is the equivalent of our English 'Smith'). He chatted to us all the way and insisted on referring to me as Mr Lob. I figured that the Korean people must have problems pronouncing 'r', so I said nothing. That is, until Mr Kim turned his attention to Lew, or should I say 'Rew'. My theory foiled, we tried to correct him but it was never going to happen. So, for our entire stay, and well after we returned home, Lew was 'Rew' and I was 'Lob'. As soon as we arrived we went to the hotel restaurant. We needed good food as we had only had airline stuff for what seemed like days. We were just finishing our meal when Christopher came in saying, 'Stop eating, the Korean organisers want to take us out for a special meal!'

'When?' we asked, hoping Chris was joking. We were to be collected in just 20 minutes and we were already absolutely full.

No sooner had we arrived at the restaurant than a procession of waiters began delivering tray after tray of food that I could not even vaguely recognise. I had also been told, much to my horror, that a Korean delicacy was live monkey brains. They apparently put a monkey in a cage under the table . . . you'll have to imagine the rest as I can't bring myself to describe it. As the food was being brought in I kept looking under the table and was very relieved to see no cages, anywhere! The food though, just kept on coming. Our hosts wanted to give us everything we could possibly need, and then some, to make our stay as happy as possible. We were seated at a round, multi-tiered table and beside each of us sat the Korean equivalent of a geisha. It was her job to hand-feed us every morsel of our abundant meal. I was still so full from our first dinner that I began to panic. I had to think fast — how was I to lighten this load without seeming rude?

I asked if it were considered wrong to ask the girls to eat with us and thankfully our interpreter smiled and said, 'If you wish so, invite them.' That, of course, meant that, first, they were not feeding us and, second, they would eat some of the food for us. We were in a private dining room so it took us quite by surprise when some musicians arrived and set up near us. They began to play, then a couple of singers arrived and we were soon treated to a floor show. Great, we thought, another distraction from the food. We applauded and when silence fell our interpreter whispered, 'Now it's your turn.' Stephen and I had to sing for our supper and we were totally unprepared. We really only knew his contest song together but we stood up — very slowly, as we were so full by now that we could barely move — and made our way over to the musicians. We wound up singing the Lionel Ritchie song, 'Three Times a Lady', and went to sit down again only to find our path was blocked. They wanted more, so we sang. . . . I can't remember how many more songs we did that night, but just as we thought we could stand up no longer, we were whisked away to our waiting car. Mr Kim was there to explain to us that Seoul was under a curfew and everyone had to be off the streets by 10.30 p.m. The time at that moment was 10.10 p.m. and we had miles and miles to get to the hotel. Our driver turned out to be a whizz at the wheel. We ran red lights, dodged through traffic and made it safely back to our hotel with just moments to spare. So dazzled by the sudden finish to our evening and the lightning dash home, we laughed and laughed for ages. We did make a note, though, to check our schedule carefully every day — this was obviously a curfew to take seriously!

Being a camera buff I photographed everything, but just as I was getting quite carried away with my photo-essay on Korea, they called a halt to my shutter-bugging. We were in a very tall building, and all the north-facing windows were blocked out, cameras not allowed. It turned out that the North Korean border was way too visible from any location with height and I guess they didn't want anyone photographing their military installations. You couldn't really blame them.

We'd been told, on the day before the big event, that we would have a dress rehearsal, but with such short notice and 18 countries involved, it seemed impossible to organise. While we went into a tailspin the Koreans treated me very well. The local tailor had stood me on something akin to a 'lazy Susan' and, with chalk and tape measures flying, fitted me for a tuxedo. This suit was to be delivered to the centre on show night — the following day. Later that day I was to perform on my first Korean television show, and went to have my make-up done. I was seated between a bunch of Korean actors who were shooting their local drama/soap. While I sat being painted, I was amused watching their (very violent) show coming together, segment by segment. When I was done, I looked in the mirror and nearly fell off my chair — I was bright orange! They had applied my make-up with a trowel, and while it may have been a perfect colour for balancing the Korean skin tone for television, it made me look positively ill. I had no desire to offend them so I waited for an appropriate moment and removed the lot in my dressing room and started again.

The show and the interview went well, and with the promise of a suit on the night I went into the rehearsal for the contest in a pair of jeans and a Toronto Maple Leafs' (hockey team) shirt. The room was otherwise filled with people dressed to kill, but nobody said a word, everyone was so polite. They were still polite on the night of the main event, when they handed me an album of songs which had been recorded at the dress rehearsal. The album sleeve had a glorious photo of everyone in frocks and tuxedos and me, in my jeans and shirt . . . oops . . . go the Maples!

The theatre complex held around 5000 people and it seemed that every one of them was in the mood to yell support — it was phenomenal. I was floored when they honoured me with the Performer's Trophy and we were told that we had been extremely close to winning the Grand Prix

— the combination of Performer and Song prizes. The song prize actually went to Korea. As we left the theatre, the 5000 people inside swelled to 10,000 with 15,000 outside, and all were totally hyped. The contest had been televised and I reckon everyone from within a 25-km radius had come to cheer at the theatre door. I was one of the last to come outside and the crowd was a tremendous shock, the noise was deafening. The organisers had provided us with a bus to get all the performers to our hotel, but as I looked out into the night I could barely see the thing. It was parked some 100 m away and to get to it I was going to have to navigate my way through the sea of screaming people, all flailing their arms about in excitement. Out of nowhere two little Korean policemen lifted me by the arms and virtually carried me towards the bus. People started reaching out, things were becoming weird. The crowd surged towards us and I became aware that I'd lost Lew, Chris and Stephen somewhere behind me. Police around me started drawing their batons as people yelled louder and began to push towards the bus. The police escorted me all the way to the bus, holding back the crowd as we went. With one song I had gained celebrity status — unbelievable. Once aboard the bus I saw that Lew and everyone else had managed to get there safely too, and just as the bus began to rock back and forth with the force of the mob, the driver began the slow process of driving off through the crowd. Visiting Korea was a great experience. As I mentioned earlier, it was a real eye-opener, but I was happy to be on my way back to New Zealand, where at least I knew what I was eating!

The trophy I was awarded was called the FIDOF Award, by the Federation of Song Contest organisers. This prize included an invitation to perform in Prague, Czechoslovakia. I was booked, alongside Shirley Bassey and the Three Degrees, to perform five songs as a guest artist at the Federation's International Song Contest. So, I was away again. The flight to Prague would take us over the Middle East, and as I sat in my comfortable seat 36,000 ft above the desert I watched in horror as I saw the tracer fire from countless missiles finding their marks. It seemed so surreal — here I was watching a movie and having dinner when just below us people were fighting a never-ending war, giving and losing their lives for their beliefs. It also struck me that had they wanted to, it wouldn't have taken too much to make us part of the nightmare in our commercial jet. I travelled with Lew and Freddy Hemara, who was also going along to perform in the contest, and together we endured the incredibly long flight and another huge culture shock. We had been warned not to take too many pieces of expensive electronic equipment, such as cameras or tape decks, as they were likely to disappear as we went through Customs. Prague is a city that Hitler didn't flatten, and although it was bitterly cold, it was stunningly beautiful. The buildings have abundant character, the city is punctuated with gold domes, threaded with cobblestoned streets, and ornate bridges span the river in elegant arches.

Once again, looking for some of the comforts of home, we stayed in a Western-style hotel. On the morning of our second day, Freddy, Lew and I went down to breakfast and when our waiter arrived we ordered something like muesli, toast, scrambled eggs and coffee. The chap gave us a puzzled look and suggested, in very broken English, 'Ham and eggs.' We all looked at each other and just nodded. After a while a plate was put in front of each of us; our ham and eggs had arrived, all mixed together, looking like a mad dog's dinner. We laughed and ate our breakfast, and this same fare was then served to us for breakfast every day, no matter what we tried to order from the menu.

We visited a local circus and by the time the show had finished, the temperature had dropped to 10 degrees below. We bolted back to our cosy hotel where I ordered cognac for our interpreter,

Freddy and Lew. I was told that I had just spent the equivalent of a local's weekly wage, which I found upsetting.

Rehearsals for the concert went well but I have no idea what happened to Shirley Bassey. The concert was to run for around two and a half hours and a portion of this was to be televised to a population of more than 400 million! On the night of the concert, unbeknown to the performers, the satellite link failed. The show started regardless and the local TV audience were treated to at least half of this internationally sponsored show, exclusively. When we were about halfway through the show — as luck would have it, during my first number — the satellite kicked back in. They told me later that since it had dropped out again during my fourth song I was the only performer who had actually been beamed live! If Shirley had been there I don't think she would have been too happy. The next day as I walked through Prague, heads turned and people stopped me to ask for my autograph. The power of television is really very spooky. The next time we went to breakfast I found my status had changed there too. I arrived before Freddy and Lew and settled down to endure my ham and eggs, but as the waiter arrived (we had the same one every day) I noticed that his surly demeanour had disappeared and so had my ham and eggs. In their place he carried a bowl of delicious-looking muesli and some hot, crisp toast with fluffy scrambled eggs. Sadly for Lew and Freddy, after they'd spent a moment or two getting excited about my breakfast, their 'ham and eggs' arrived as usual. I couldn't help but laugh . . . aaahh television. . . .

On the way back to New Zealand we stopped off in London to catch up on a few new shows. One that I particularly wanted to see was *Barnum*, starring Michael Crawford. I had just been signed to do this show with Robert Young, in Wanganui, so I was hoping to compare some ideas with Michael. I got my chance and made the most of some valuable time with him, unaware, of course, that our paths would regularly cross from then on.

As I headed home I considered in depth the fact that people had so often asked me why I have chosen such a gypsy existence. 'What about security?' they'd ask. 'What about stability?' I think the way they are programmed makes them believe that in order to be happy they need a regular job. I figured it may have been time to test their theory. My passion has always been (apart from my family, of course, and my cars) photography, so I decided that photography should be the nature of my 'regular' business. I found premises in Auckland and had the interior slightly remodelled to suit my purpose. I bought all the photography gear I needed and with the idea of concentrating on portfolios, model shots and product brochures, I had stationery printed and opened the doors. I loved working with the camera in my hand, I thoroughly enjoyed the whole creative process but, frankly, the behind the scenes, practical, everyday stuff bored me to death. Thankfully, I was still doing fairly regular performance work so I could justify hiring a young photographer, Stephen Edwards, to run the studio for me. My mother helped too, by running the studio reception desk. We managed to land contracts to shoot product brochures for a couple of well-known retailers and this provided us with our base income. I went away when necessary to perform, but remained as involved with the studio as possible. After the first year I bought a property and built a studio from scratch. I enjoyed this regular business but soon realised that you can't really run one well without being there. Even though I'd even built a studio, in the end I was either going to have to stop performing (simply NOT an option) or shut up shop. It was a sad day indeed, but I had to close those doors.

I will never regret taking the time for my day job, as it taught me so much and helped to balance my perspective on life. Another gem of my father's wisdom was, 'You shouldn't make your hobby your living, because in the end you'll lose a precious hobby.' So, I took back my hobby and my dream.

Lynette at this stage was firmly committed to the Auckland Rugby Union as she was staging special events for their matches using a new attraction — cheerleaders. Again we were ships passing in the night and so, after almost eight years, Lynette and I called it quits . . . this time for good.

As the *Barnum* opening drew closer I found myself back in the old rehearsal room. Once again Robert Young was there, working his wizardry to help me bring PT Barnum to life. In general I knew what to expect, having seen the show in London, but actually performing the tricks was quite a different thing altogether. I had many challenging skills to learn — they needed me to be able to walk a tightrope, hang from trapezes, tumble and juggle. All this, along with mastering the intricacies of the songs, dialogue and stage movements kept me extremely busy, and I loved it. I was hardly off the stage for the whole show, and while this was a great, fun character role, I think I discovered a new bruise every day. Man, did those tricks bite! *Barnum* was a huge success and predictably other centres wanted to stage the show. Luckily, they also wanted me to play the lead. First in the queue was Dunedin, but with plenty of time before *Barnum* was to head off I signed a deal to play Danny Zuko in a production of *Grease*.

This was a windfall opportunity to work again with Anne Pilkinton, who is still one of my dearest friends. A wonderful musical director, Anne had helped me through many previous shows and we always managed to have a load of fun. *Grease* was a new show for both of us and it turned out to be our world-shaker. We had been rehearsing in Kawerau for about a week when Anne and I went to do an interview with a local newspaper. The rest of the cast had been rehearsing for months and we had just one week left before opening. So, between rehearsals with the show's director, David Rossitor, putting the pieces together and trying the odd variation, I was trying to fit in a few publicity appearances.

On this occasion, Anne remained in the car while I dashed in for my interview at the paper. Suddenly and without warning the building started to shake. Books were falling from their shelves, the shelves then started to tear off the walls, desks were jiggling about and people began to scream and run from the building. As the building steadied and the reality of what was happening dawned on me, I ran to see what had become of Anne in the car. Sure enough Anne was still in the car, but the car was no longer where I had parked it, it had been shaken sideways and across the car park by the quake. I pulled the shaking Anne from the car and we crossed the street. A motorbike shop next to us had all of its bikes knocked over and the owner was busily trying to stand them all up again, when the second quake hit. People were screaming once more, so we barely heard one chap yell at us to move. When we realised he was signalling to us, we looked up to see we were sitting under a high-voltage power line which was swaying, dangerously close to collapse. Needless to say, he did not have to tell us again!

A veterinarian appeared at that point, carrying a dog he had been operating on. I went over to help him as the poor dog, a large black labrador, was obviously distraught. The vet was also carrying a bottle of something alcoholic and he started offering it around saying, in a broad Scottish accent, 'Take a swig, it'll do yeh good!' I recall saying out loud, 'Oh my God, it must be the end of the world if the Scots are giving away the booze!'

It was a long time before we felt we could return to the car. The air was filled with the sound of piercing sirens and bellowing horns. Most of the animals had long ago taken to the hills, and it would be days in some instances before they returned to their homes. We heard a little while later that the main earthquake had registered 7.5 on the Richter scale and that the epicentre had been in the sea by White Island. Poor old Edgecumbe had apparently borne the brunt of its energy. Kawerau was largely cut off. The roads into town all crossed bridges at some point and most of these bridges had dropped by a foot or more. So, it was a couple of days before we could get out to see how Edgecumbe had fared. When we got there, we were shocked — it resembled a war zone. Train tracks had been twisted and buckled, buildings split down the middle, and many residents were left homeless. We returned to Kawerau, where we were grateful that the damage was mostly restricted to roofs; and once tarpaulins had been cast about, we were OK. *Grease*, of course, would have to wait. They put us on hold for a week, and we all began the clean-up.

Immediately after the inital quake there were hundreds of aftershocks, which frightened everyone with the thought that there might be another big one. Many locals, too nervous to return to their homes, slept on Anne's living-room floor, and I set up a bar from the boot of my car and offered distressed people a calming brandy. It did seem to steady their shaking, but conversation was generally still panicky. Many people were too afraid to go inside, so they paced around outside, worrying about family members they hadn't sighted yet, a variety of lost pets and much broken property. The night came too quickly for many. About 30 people spread out on Anne's lounge floor, in almost total darkness as we were without power. I found a torch, showed everyone how to get out if there was another big quake, then took myself off to bed. At about 3 a.m. I woke to more loud screaming and shouting. I staggered sleepily through the house but couldn't find anybody. Out on the lawn the crowd had gathered and as I yawned the question, 'What's all the fuss about?' they all started at once. It seemed I had taken the only torch to my room and I'd slept through another large earthquake. In the meantime, everyone else had been jolted awake, panicked and fumbled about in the dark, looking for the torch . . . oops.

The local authorities had effectively cordoned off the whole area to sightseers because of the unsafe roads. In fact, they were not letting anyone in beyond the outskirts of Rotorua. As a result, when my good mate Phil Parkinson, who was to arrange the sound on *Grease*, tried to get in they blocked his way. None of us within the boundary were supposed to be driving around either, but as soon as there was a road I felt was stable enough, I made the drive, very carefully, out to get him.

The show finally opened to an audience who were very ready for an entertaining distraction. When my character, Danny, spoke his first words, which happened to be, 'Hey you guys, what's shaking?' the audience erupted with laughter and they loudly chorused 'KAWERAU!' We were off to a great start and the season never had a flat moment.

With *Grease* finished I made my way to Dunedin, ready to recreate *Barnum*. I was looking forward to it with only one reservation: Robert was not directing this time. Rex Simpson had been directing the rehearsals and things were bound to be a little different. My arrival at the airport held no surprises. I was driven to the hotel to drop off my belongings and whisked away again to watch the rehearsal. This was the first time I had been back to Dunedin to do a show since I had lost Dad, and it brought back many memories.

I walked into the hall and was introduced to the beautiful Judy Barnes; she was to play my wife, Charity Barnum. I remember her slipping straight into character when she saw me and saying, 'You've been away a long time.' I responded, also in character, with the next line, 'Yeah, yeah, well, I've been busy!' We hit it off immediately. The news came in that Rex Simpson had been in a dreadful car accident and he was badly injured. As he was to be hospitalised for a long time, the show was to be given a new director. The new guy was thrown in at the deep end, since the characters were forming and most of the stage direction had been set. He knew that if he needed to make changes, he had to do it fast and we all had to adapt quickly. Rehearsals as a result were long and tiring, but the show did come together, and surprisingly well. Judy had recently played the lead in *The Boyfriend* and was proving to be perfect as Charity Barnum. The show had a terrific season and I managed to dodge any serious injuries, but not everyone was so lucky.

At the end of the first act, I had a particularly spectacular exit to make. As I hit the final note, sitting on a trapeze, I had to let myself fall backwards, turning my feet out from the ankles so they would catch the seat. Two crew members would haul me swiftly, upside down, toward the 'fly-floor' some 20 m above. While I sang the big note, six fire-eaters would blow a ball of fire skyward in unison, and I would disappear 'in flame'. The curtain would then close on Act I.

One night, things did not go according to plan. In fact it all went terribly wrong. Peter Turner, one of the fire-eaters, had managed to dribble some of his highly flammable liquid onto his costume, which was made of lycra. As the flame came back at him he became a ball of fire instantly. From my precarious position, upside down hanging above the stage, I could hear screaming, and craning my neck I watched, unable to help as the cast and all available crew tried to help him. I must admit, the thought did occur to me that all the crew, including the two firemen who were supposed to pull me to safety, may have been distracted by the events on stage and forget to haul me up and off my trapeze. I needn't have worried, they were there and they helped me get to the walkway and down the ladder before they took off to help Peter. We visited him in hospital the next day, and while he was still in a lot of pain from his burns he seemed, remarkably, well on the way to recovery. I'm still in contact with Peter and I'm pleased to say he is still a driving force in theatre in Dunedin.

Accidents like that are rare, thank goodness, but in those days we did take a lot more risks than perhaps we should have. I recall in one production jumping on a flying fox from the top floor of a theatre and flying over an audience as pyrotechnics exploded below. This would never be allowed today for many reasons, not the least of which is because it obviously puts the patrons in danger. Still, this sort of thing makes one hell of an entrance! Remember my early childhood mania with danger? I guess I never outgrew it.

Having done eight shows a week for as long as I have, I have learned that Murphy's Law is not a myth — if something can go wrong, believe me it will. I've mentioned before some of my animal antics . . . well, inanimate objects are just as deadly. It's just a matter of time before that simple prop will undo you. It could be a letter you have to read on stage that's sealed with wax which just won't come undone (*Les Miserables*), or an apple that has a mind of its own (*The Phantom of the Opera*), or a cigarette that won't go out (*Grease*). The list could go on and on — the trick is not to let it throw you. Sometimes these objects have been known to get a helping hand to bring you undone. In Kawerau, while playing Joseph in the season's last performance of *Joseph and the Amazing Technicolor Dreamcoat*, the final scene proved slippery. The 'dreamcoat' was lowered to the stage from the 'flys' and put on me, as usual, by the willing hands of the cast. This time someone had completely filled the sleeves with Vaseline. As I was pretty much naked from the waist up I felt every ounce of the cold, slimy grease and it caught me totally by surprise. It felt weird and disgusting and keeping my composure was not easy, but . . . I know who was responsible . . . Craig Pilkinton . . . lucky you're a mate. All good, sometimes clean, fun as long as the audience don't catch on. I guess maybe I've invited you all to watch a little harder now.

One of the most interesting things about live theatre is the fact that the human element is always right at hand. You can work on a piece, honing it for weeks, months, even years until you really feel you've 'nailed it', yet every night, within the realms of direction, your character will be slightly different. You are trying to portray a character, and to make them truly believable you have to 'become' them as much as possible. The person, or people, playing opposite you are doing the same thing with their character, so it makes sense that, between all of you on stage, someone or something will occasionally happen not quite as it was scripted.

It may happen that you drop a line. As we don't use prompts if you lose a line, no one can help you! If you do, the person on stage with you has to make a lightning-fast decision — either they follow the scene to where you've led it and hope to retrieve the thread of the story, or they run for the hills. Thank heavens it's usually the former, but in musicals without dialogue this is not possible as the music dictates everything. Miss a line and it's gone.

This situation is at its worst when the block of dialogue you've just dumped contains information vital to the plot. I've been known to attempt to retrieve the important bits while my cast members stand by, white-knuckled, waiting for the moment they have to pick up their line, all the while listening for how they may need to alter it to maintain a meaningful dialogue. Tricky!

6.

Hey Jude

BARNUM WAS A DIFFICULT show, unyielding in its demands — physically, vocally and emotionally. I thought I'd seen it all, but how wrong could I have been? If only I'd had a crystal ball. I left Dunedin after a very successful season and began mentally preparing myself to, once again, play Danny Zuko for the Tokoroa production of *Grease*. I was reaching the point in my career where I felt I needed more. Not on stage — I've never been anything but in my element there — I mean I wanted to be more involved in the creative process. I started to dream of directing my first stage production. In the back of my mind, I knew it would mean handing over the reins. Someone else would get to do the actual performing, but I figured I would face that demon when it arose. So, with some positive feedback from industry associates, I began investigating the art of direction.

Judy Barnes who played my wife, Charity, in *Barnum* had been in Australia on a club tour, working at all the major Sydney clubs. We had kept in touch and she came to visit me on her return to New Zealand. The call that would change the direction of my life came while Judy was there. Cameron Mackintosh, Australia, were in New Zealand to audition for the Australian production of *Les Miserables*. I had listened to the CD of the production and I loved it. I knew, however, that the only two roles that truly captured my interest were taken — that of Valjean, which was being played by Normie Rowe, and the role of Javert, by Philip Quast. So when Judy told me she had actually seen the Australian production and thought it was wonderful, I was torn. Why bother auditioning? I remained undecided — right up until the morning of the meeting when Lew called to check that I was still planning to go.

Jude and I talked it through. She basically said, 'What have you got to lose?' and I remember saying that I had been really looking forward to a change of direction. Her argument was just too compelling, so off I went to the Town Hall. I met John Robertson, executive producer for Cameron Mackintosh in Australia, and the musical director for *Les Miserables*, Peter Casey. As I left the house I had picked up a piece of music, with barely a glance to see what it was. This I handed to the rehearsal pianist and, as she started to play, Peter walked over and took charge. He asked if I had heard the score of *Les Miserables* and passed me a piece of music. It was Valjean's soliloquy. I sang for him, and next he gave me the prayer, 'Bring Him Home'. After I'd sung, John and Peter followed me outside and John asked me if I could be in Sydney on the following Tuesday. What do you think I said?

I flew to Australia to work with Gale Edwards, the show's director. I was still somewhat in the dark as to their intentions because, as far as I was concerned, those two most interesting roles were spoken for. Even so, between the meeting in Auckland and the trip to Sydney I worked on the material they had given me. It was Valjean. I arrived in Sydney and stayed at the Sebel Townhouse. On the morning of my first day with Gale I took the chance to walk to the Theatre Royal, in order to try to get my head in the right place. When I arrived, Wayne Jelly escorted me to the green-room, where I waited to be called. I could hear other people working on the show but the muffled sounds gave me no idea that they, also, were working on Valjean material with Gale. When my turn came, I worked for an hour or so, going through my paces on the set of the legendary *Les Miserables*. It was both an exhilarating and nerve-wracking experience. When it was over, I had a very bland meeting with John and he said that they were very pleased with the day. They thanked me for everything, explained that there was nothing available for me at that moment and said they would keep in touch. I watched the performance that night and was totally enthralled, it was brilliant.

I walked back to the hotel and the next day I flew back to Auckland, where Jude met me at the airport. Naturally, she asked me what had happened and I barely knew what to say. 'Nothing', was eventually my response. I didn't know whether I should feel sad at missing this opportunity, or happy that I would be free to pursue my directing career. It did seem to have been a wasted trip. Two days later, Lew called to say that Matthew Dalco, the production coordinator for Cameron Mackintosh in Australia, had called to ask if I could be in Sydney within 48 hours. They wanted me to take over the position of alternate for Valjean, which meant I would play the lead role once a week, and full time for a period of three weeks, while Normie took a holiday. They made me an offer I could not refuse, so I packed up my belongings and went back to Sydney.

During the season that we played Charity and PT in *Barnum*, Jude and I became very good friends and working together had been a gift. When the show closed neither of us had any idea that we would meet again, but as the days went by and Jude spent time in Australia, we both became aware that what we had together was very, very special. We missed each other, and once Jude had returned to New Zealand we decided to start this new adventure together, in Sydney. We were packed and ready to go, Jude was in the car and I was doing the final checks through the house to make sure nothing had been left behind. We were booked into a hotel for the night as we were due to fly the next day. The check completed, I turned out the light and walked into the side of the open door, leading with my head — ouch! Wondering what was taking so long, Jude came to investigate and found me concussed and bloodied. This was not good for our plans. . . . We had to make a couple of urgent calls across the Tasman to explain that I couldn't fly and it was another two days before we left for Australia.

We found a small apartment in Double Bay and as the days went by Jude and I grew closer and closer. I was so glad to have her support as the long vocal rehearsals were exhausting. Preparing for a show like *Les Miserables* is a meticulous process — every word is sung and the score is the Bible . . . never shall one deviate from it! The pressure was really on to pick up things quickly as the American who had been working as the alternate, JC Sheets, was rapidly running out of visa time and had to leave the country.

I made a habit of singing the entire show every day to learn the whole thing and most importantly, to become 'show fit'. It is a very demanding piece vocally and I am thankful I had many years of experience to call on. So, I practised and rehearsed, and though it seemed like an eternity before I could take to the stage, the reality was it was only six weeks. I loved playing the role of Valjean — the only problem was I had to keep giving it back. That was never easy to do, and once again it was Jude who kept me sane. She would let me air my frustration at having to sit around and perform only once a week. We spent three months in that little apartment and then Jude gave me the wonderful news that she was expecting our baby. We decided to look for a bigger place to live and eventually found a little three-bedroom house in Lane Cove, on the North Shore. We also decided to invite Mum to live with us as she was on her own in Auckland. She accepted and we all moved in together.

In the meantime, as far as work was concerned I was going stir-crazy. I asked the producers if I could learn the role of Javert. I was allowed, and I even went on in the role for one performance. This gave me an amazing insight into both characters, which was to hold me in good stead for the times to come.

During these early days I became very good friends with the *Les Miserables* company manager, Andrew Pain. We both have a passion for cars and we spent many an hour comparing notes. I even remember travelling to Wollongong to purchase a Lotus with him. I think this particular car, though, is one he would rather forget.

On 4 January 1989, life as I knew it was to change, forever. Judy gave birth to our son, Christopher John (John after my father). I recall the day so very well, probably not as vividly as Jude, of course, but WOW! We left home at about 1.30 a.m. for the hospital, and Chris, setting his own pace (nothing has changed) was born later that morning at 10.45. I remember the midwife asking me, 'What is it?' and me, in shock, wanting to say, 'It's a baby, you idiot', but I managed to control myself just in time to say, quite reasonably, 'It's a boy.'

This singular moment was the most astonishing in my life. I witnessed a miracle in the birth of my son. He was beautiful, with a shock of red hair (compliments of Jude's grandmother) and a serene little face. I bathed him and carried him down the corridor while I sang to him. He was all ours. I counted his toes and fingers, and I couldn't stop kissing and holding him, even though I will admit now that I was terrified. Jude was doing well and had a glow about her that matched the beauty of our son. My son . . . Wow! I left the hospital at around 4 p.m. and stopped at a garage to get milk and bread. On my way back to the car, in my euphoria, I tripped over the gutter and landed, very ungracefully, taking a chunk out of my knee and grazing both elbows. I looked around to see if anyone had noticed. Funny how we do that . . . then I limped back to the car. The peak-hour traffic crawled up the highway and when I finally reached home, some time later, I found there had been a phone call. They had called me in to do the show! That night, of all nights, with no sleep and bruises all over but I didn't really care. You see . . . I had a son!

The show that night was wonderful. Something lifted me through it; that is until 'Bring Him Home'. This moved me so deeply that I found it incredibly hard not to let my built-up emotions take control. I made it, but this prayer was to prove very difficult to perform many times thereafter. The next morning, armed with flowers and a teddy dressed in blue I headed back to the hospital. When I saw him, this second day of his sweet life, I realised that I hadn't simply had a wonderful dream. He really did exist. Then all the questions flooded into my mind. What did the future hold for him? Was I going to be a good and fair father? I would love him, I knew that, and I would protect, guide and care for him, that I also knew. What a responsibility! A new little life in our hands . . .

Nothing can prepare you for becoming a parent. There is no manual. No 'quick fix' course or 'how to' video. It's all up to you and you just have to learn to trust and follow your instincts. When I put him in the car, with Jude, to take them home from the hospital, the notion of all this responsibility, the reality of having to take care of this little miracle, truly hit home. I guess I probably found it a little more overwhelming than Jude, as she had been with Christopher every day. This was a new challenge for me. With no more nursing staff to help, whatever he ate, drank, everything, was over to us. He was a little angel and we discovered quickly that he would let us know if he needed something, by crying, loudly, whenever he was tired, hungry or 'uncomfortable'. I know every new parent experiences this, but I guess you don't fully understand the enormity of it until you become one.

With my life and focus changed completely, the early days of *Les Miserables* were much easier. We never missed the chance to spend time with Chris. Suddenly my life was even fuller than I could have imagined and every day we were rewarded tenfold. I did a three-week run as Valjean but it only made it harder to give the role back. I had never been in this position before. I had had quite enough of sitting around and so I told the powers that be that I would be leaving at the end of my current contract.

The show was due to close in Sydney and the next stop was to be Melbourne. Unsure of quite why, I was flown to Melbourne with the other principals for the press launch.

Then it happened. I was asked to take over the role of Valjean for the Melbourne production.

**With Philip Quast.
Opening night,
Les Miserables,
Adelaide, 1991.**

All that waiting had paid off, though it was a little bitter-sweet because Normie had apparently had some problem with management, the result of which was a parting of the ways for them and management replacing him with me. Cameron then had me flown to New York to work with Bob Billig who, at the time, was the musical director for the Broadway *Les Miserables* production and also musical supervisor, worldwide, for the show. Bob was wonderful and so generous in spirit. We worked from his Manhattan apartment and I sat in at a rehearsal and saw the Broadway production with him conducting that night. JC Sheets, the guy I had replaced originally in Sydney, was playing Valjean, and covering the role for Tim Shew on this occasion. The show was great, as I believe it will always be as it's such a great story. I did have a slight problem with the American accents but I still thought it was wonderful.

The following day I saw a matinee of Jerome Robbins' *Broadway*, which was awe-inspiring, and that night a newish show on Broadway, *The Phantom of the Opera*. I was blown away by the fantastic set, the costumes and the story — it was spectacular. Once again, if only I'd had a crystal ball. . . . I was only in New York for about three days and then I flew to London for, believe it or not, a costume fitting. It was becoming clear that when the Cameron Mackintosh organisation does something, they do it right!

While in London, I visited Cameron in his offices and was given a tour of a new show called *Miss Saigon* that they were opening in two weeks. I also caught the West End production of *Les Miserables* in which my good friend Philip Quast was playing Inspector Javert. He was brilliant and for my money stole the show. He had left the Aussie production while it was still in Sydney, to take up the role in London, and professionally he has never looked back. My stay in London included the obligatory tour of the city. I had seen it all many times but I was 13 when I left. Funny how Nelson's Column hadn't changed a bit. Just a few more pigeons. As soon as I returned home we packed up house and moved to Melbourne where we set up home again in the suburb of Malvern.

The *Les Miserables* rehearsals were held in a place called Ormond Hall and it turned out that our rehearsal period was to be extended and our opening night delayed because the Princess Theatre was not ready for us. The builders were running behind schedule on a multimillion-dollar refurbishment. So, we rehearsed and rehearsed, day after day, until one day we caused the revolve to crash through the floor of the rehearsal hall. It was a good job we were almost out of there, as I don't think the old place was up to much more of us. We had a dream cast and if you look at the people in *Les Miserables* back then, you realise they now make up the backbone of Australian musical theatre.

Bob came out from New York to oversee our transition. It was great to catch up again and a good chance to get another opinion on this monster role. He was always full of praise for the work done by Peter Casey and Gale Edwards and, 10 years later, it was my turn to understand how grateful I was for them too. We moved into the theatre — there was dust everywhere. The dressing rooms weren't completed and members of the cast were changing in a motel over the road. The principals shared dressing rooms as there weren't enough to go around. I shared with Anthony Warlow, who was playing the student Enjolras, and these were fun times. Shortly before we were due to open I was hit with a throat virus. All the rehearsals and the long, long hours had done nothing, I'd been fine, and now . . . WHAM! Well, nothing was going to prevent me from being there on opening night so I fought hard. I rested my throat, steamed and did everything possible, until at last I knew I could do it. I made it to opening night — and what a fantastic night it was. *LES MISERABLES* HAD ARRIVED IN MELBOURNE!

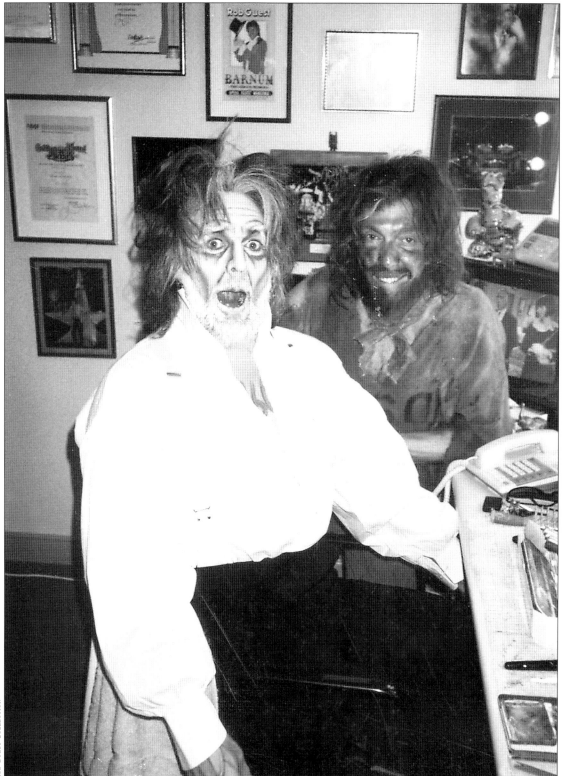

Opening night is always special with all the fanfare, the well-wishers, the opening night gifts, flowers and the electricity backstage. Once opening night is behind you, that is when the real work begins. It is the ongoing nature of theatre that separates the men from the boys. I have always said that there are many talented people out there who can sing a lead in a major musical, and there is probably an equal number who could act it. There is a limited number who could do both, and a number smaller still who could then set about doing it for eight shows a week, and love every minute of it! You see, it's not just the time in the spotlight, it's the publicity calls, the rehearsals that keep on going until all hours, the travelling, the note sessions. All of these things take their toll, if you let them. At this point you may well ask what it is that I think makes me different, enables me to do this stuff. The answer is simple — I would not want to be anywhere else. I wouldn't want to be doing anything else. My family kept me grounded and sane and they, through their generosity and understanding, allowed me to do what I believe I was destined to do. I must perform.

Les Miserables in Melbourne was a hit. You couldn't beg, borrow or steal a ticket anywhere. The catchphrase for our publicity was 'Fight to Get a Ticket', and people, when they could, were seeing the show two or three times. We worked very hard at keeping the show fresh while telling the story as we had been directed. We had terrific backup, which is one of the other wonderful benefits of being in a 'Cam Mac' show — the show and all its people are looked after incredibly well. A resident director is always watching the show and a musical supervisor always listening. So, the feedback performers receive on a day-to-day basis is invaluable. The process of honing a role and fine-tuning each aspect is constant, and I look at it as a 'work in progress'. There is always an opportunity to improve.

When I started at the Princess Theatre I was introduced to someone who was to play a huge part in my life and career for the next eight years. I walked into my dressing room and there he was, hanging my costumes on a rack and tidying up. He was to be my dresser, Norman Goodman. I felt as if I'd known him all my life, his credentials were impeccable and I don't think there are many people in this industry that he hasn't looked after. He'd worked everywhere from Covent Garden to New Zealand on tour. He was not purely my assistant, he became my very good friend, a member of my family. Fiercely loyal, he would protect my privacy, yet still get me to undertake some of the tedious chores that others would never dream of approaching me with. Norman had an abiding love for the Princess and spent much of his time researching this amazing theatre with its owners, Elaine and David Marriner. He used to tell me stories about the resident ghost, Federici, and, I must say, I experienced a few unexplained moments for myself during the *Les Miserables* run there. They used to say that the smell of toast backstage was a sure sign that something supernatural was about. I don't know about that but I have met many performers who swear that they have experienced unexplained phenomena there. On one occasion the front of house staff were amused to see me in full Valjean military uniform, standing at the back of the audience watching the show. As they watched the stage, I appeared over the barricade. Quickly looking back to where I had been standing they realised that I had gone — the problem is, I had never been there in the first place. I would never go into the audience during a production unless it was part of the show. There is no explanation for this unexpected appearance. Perhaps Federici was looking for a few pointers.

Opposite page: Hamming it up for the camera after the show with Norman, who had dressed up as me as Valjean . . . complicated?

Right: Closing night —
Les Miserables,
Melbourne, 1990.

Opposite page: A clever
photo trick. Two photos —
one in rehearsal and one
in dress rehearsal of the
same scene, end of Act I,
singing 'One Day More',
Les Miserables.

And so the myth continues . . . fact, or fiction? I would love to believe it was for real, but then I'm just an old romantic.

Norman really made my dressing room a home away from home. Couches were brought in, framed photos adorned the walls, pot plants were everywhere, a television in the corner, fridge, coffee machine and tons of memorabilia. Norman kept it all running smoothly — what would I have done without him? One morning, as I was preparing for a matinee, putting on 'dirt' (black make-up etc.) I spotted Norman out of the corner of my eye. He was pottering about getting on with his work, but, on this occasion he was dressed exactly the same as me. He was even wearing a long wig like the one I had to wear. I collapsed laughing at his parody of me in character and he stayed dressed up that way for the whole show. He would regularly give everyone a giggle. Norman was also known for the longest 'yeeeeeeeeeeeeeeeessss' in history. If anyone called, 'Hey, Norman!' he would always respond with his trademark, 'Yeeeeeeeeeessss . . .' Three or so months into the Melbourne season, the show's management approached me with an invitation to continue to play Valjean in Perth, Adelaide, Brisbane and Auckland. Without a moment's hesitation I agreed.

The buzz that *The Phantom of the Opera* was coming to Australia was growing louder every day and notices were posted declaring that the auditions would be held on our stage at the Princess Theatre. It seemed that everyone in the industry was going to audition. Over lunch one day, John Robertson casually asked me why I wasn't auditioning for *The Phantom*. Now I need to explain that *The Phantom* was also a Cameron Mackintosh show — it was in 'the family' so to speak. I found this question a little strange as I had just agreed to tour with *Les Miserables*. While I could see no point in auditioning, I was told that Hal Prince, the director of *The Phantom*, should at

least see me, so I agreed. I prepared 'Music of the Night' and sang for the panel, not really expecting anything to come of it. Cameron met me backstage afterwards to say that a decision about who would play *The Phantom* was to be made by 4.30 p.m. that afternoon. He sounded very positive, but gave nothing away.

I really hadn't considered the possibility of playing *The Phantom* until that moment. Deep in thought, I made my way home and waited. Four-thirty came and went . . . nothing. So at 6 p.m. I headed to the theatre as usual. Cameron came to my dressing room as I was preparing for stage and asked me to tell him how much I wanted to tour with *Les Miserables*. Puzzled, I asked him to explain what he meant and he told me that he wanted me to stay with *Les Miserables* and that Anthony Warlow was to play the Phantom. I don't really know how I felt at that moment; I was happy for Anthony and I thought, 'How can I feel disappointed at not getting the role of Phantom when I am playing Valjean, and I'm about to take *Les Miserables* on tour?' It made sense to stay with *Les Miserables*, but they were both fantastic roles and it was tantalising for a moment.

Les Miserables had a further six months to play in Melbourne, so we settled down to the run. The show was a huge success and as I had opened the show in Melbourne I became known for the role. It opened many doors and I was invited to appear on more and more television shows — I was in my element! In preparation for the tour I put in a request to have Norman stay with me as my dresser and I'll always be thankful that I got my wish. I can't begin to describe how much easier my life is when my dresser is on the same wavelength as me. Norman's presence would make a world of difference on tour. He took charge of my dressing room, guarded my domain and always knew exactly where to find anything at all that I needed. Sometimes performers prefer to see their

Interval backstage Les Miserables — in my dressing room.

dresser only when they need to be dressed, and the rest of the time the dressers can be found in the hallway outside the rooms waiting until they are needed. I am not like that and I adored having the witty Norman around. His chair was always in my room and with a full view of the television, he would swivel it just perfectly, so that, still seated, he could see any visitors to my room well before they arrived. Often, he used to sense that I needed space or a little peace and he'd go to great lengths to defend my privacy.

The time came for *Les Miserables* to move to its new home at Her Majesty's Theatre, Perth. The hard-working crew were set to work around the clock to make it happen — when a show the size of this one makes a move, it is a major logistical nightmare. I was always astonished to find that, after each move, I could arrive at the new theatre in the new city and find that Norman had recreated my 'home away from home' in my dressing room. Not only that, but the amazing crew had recreated everything else, just as we had left it in the last city. The set would be up, the stage marked out, and the lighting focused. All the cast had to do was get used to the sight-lines of the new theatre and we were up and running. I found this feat remarkable. These people were the best in the business and I am still lucky enough to count many from this show, and other fabulous crews with whom I've worked, as close friends.

During the last few weeks of the Melbourne season I flew to Perth to look for appropriate accommodation, as the Guest clan were about to hit the road. After an exhausting search I found a house that was perfect — I couldn't believe how well it all fell into place. The owners were about to go overseas and the timing could not have been better. We had just discovered that Jude was expecting another baby, and Christopher was of course crawling by this time and into absolutely everything. So, it was a little difficult when we realised I had overlooked a few (minor) obstacles, such as the fact that every door (or so it seemed) opened onto the home's gorgeous swimming pool. Also, that the house was furnished in white. White walls, white furniture and white carpet. This was every parent's nightmare. We lived with locked doors and furniture covers everywhere.

The view, overlooking the Swan River, was fantastic and the sunsets were stunning, so I enjoyed them while I could. I knew that, while we (the cast) were taking a break from our eight shows a week, resting our voices, mending all the bruises and tired muscles, huge road trucks were roaring across the Nullabor Plain bringing our little piece of France to Perth. The move to Perth was a monster, and a huge task for the crew. Somehow they had to be faster than usual, moving *Les Miserables*' vast quantity of gear into a smaller theatre than we had left behind.

Love-hate relationship
with my publicist Suzie
Howie — she was
seriously trying to kill me
(just kidding)!

Rehearsals were held in the rooms above the theatre and we were put through intensive reworks as we had lost a few cast members. These sessions were vital, as *Les Miserables* is such an ensemble piece that every scene lives or dies by the detail the audience sees. There is never a moment in this great epic where you can let your guard down and be out of character. So, to prepare us, Gale really put us through our paces. We were shown a table where six pages of the great book had been copied. Gale instructed us to take one page each, and as we had a cast of 30, there were 30 copies of each page. We were asked to study a character from the page and make up a small scene involving that character. Over the rehearsal we did this six times, taking from a different pile each time, and then we put the characters all together, changing from character to character every 15 seconds. The reason for this rather elaborate exercise was to prepare everyone to play every character. All the cast, except for Valjean and the inspector, Javert, had to play multiple roles, therefore being able to change characters as quickly as discarding a costume was a very important skill. These rehearsals were amazing, and even though some of us had already been with the production for a long time, the freshness of the piece was evident. We were fired up and ready to rock. The main difference between the Princess and Her Majesty's was, for us, the sight-lines. The Maj has much steeper seating, so all our playing angles (the angle we project our faces and posture up to) needed to be pulled up, so that patrons in the upper balcony weren't looking at the tops of our heads. It is incredible how familiar things become and how habits are instilled when you have been in one place for a while.

Opening night raced up and thankfully we were ready. The show was in great shape and we all had a ball. The after-show party was, as are all Cameron Mackintosh opening night functions, extravagant to say the least. While the food looked wonderful, sadly I didn't get a mouthful as the press required interviews and photographers were chasing deadlines. My work continued late into the evening, but I had the BEST night.

The reviews were stunning and we were set to play a very full season. One reviewer, however, chose to attack the fact that Victor Hugo had not written (in his opinion) enough about the Revolution. I believe a review, be it good or bad, is one person's opinion and the public either come to see a show or they don't. So it was most unusual for me to react publicly, and I've never done it since, but I felt compelled to call this fellow's editor. I was incensed by the fact that someone had attacked Victor Hugo. If the reviewer hadn't liked my interpretation of the role, well, it might upset me for a while and I could argue against their opinion if I chose, but Victor Hugo is not here to defend himself. I explained this to the editor, that giving *Les Miserables* a hard time for not being about the French Revolution is like asking why Sir Andrew Lloyd Webber's *Cats* is not about dogs. He got my point and I had aired my opinion. I didn't want an apology, or even for him to agree with me, I just felt it was unfair to give such a wonderful work as *Les Miserables* a hard time simply in order to be different from all the other reviewers, who loved it! That one hiccup on our unblemished reputation did not hurt the box office — we were sold out for the full three-month season.

When *Les Miserables* was first performed at the Barbican Theatre in London, the press panned it, nicknaming the production 'The Glums' — this for a show that would break all box-office records worldwide. Success is surely the sweetest revenge. I almost auditioned for this original production on my way back from Prague. In fact, Lew had organised a time for me to 'be seen' by the management in London, but, as I have mentioned before, fate was to deal me a different hand. By the time the meeting had been arranged, I was already winging my way across the world. Another of life's crossroads behind me.

7.
Boating Down the Swan River

PERTH IS SUCH A beautiful city, enhanced, for me, by the wonderful Swan River. The lure was just too much for me during the hot days of summer, so I began to search for another boat. I scanned the papers for days looking for just the right boat and finally I found what I figured was a great deal. It was an 18-ft Baron with a small cabin and an outboard motor — I had to check this out. The fact that it had to be on a trailer, and would need to be towed to the water, I figured I'd deal with when and if I decided to buy it. I arrived at the boat yard and a salesman showed me the vessel I described from the paper. Sure enough it was all they had claimed, but it was also bright, bright orange and emblazoned down both sides of the hull, in huge letters, was the name *MY DINGALING*. I was so determined to get myself a boat that I tried to look beyond this and suggested that perhaps no one would notice. Yeah, right. I bought the boat and because I was a little concerned with its vintage, I purchased a small backup outboard motor for security. Now all I had to do was get it home! Back to the newspapers. I went and found myself a Ford Falcon with a nice big engine and a tow package — perfect! It would also give us a second car, which we were really beginning to need. So, I bought the car, collected the boat and went home. Once home, with a clear and constant view of the vivid hull of my new boat I realised I could not put up with *MY DINGALING*. So I took to cutting, scrubbing and polishing the signs off. Finally, after four hours, it was done, and I was happy.

That was Friday, and Sunday (our day off) seemed so far away. Finally, on Sunday morning, we packed some goodies, sandwiches and drinks and I loaded the family into the new car and we went in search of a boat ramp. We launched just out of Fremantle, and headed up the river. Judy was very pregnant, and Christopher was not yet two. There we all were, my Mum too, cruising along admiring the scenery, enjoying the glorious day, when suddenly the motor began to cough and splutter. We had been heading upriver towards our house at Dalkeith and just as our home came into view, the motor stopped. The spare outboard I'd bought made me feel very clever at that

Christopher at 2 years old, baton in hand, just looking for an orchestra.

ROB GUEST COLLECTION

moment. I threw out the anchor and headed for the stern. I pulled the starter lead and . . . nothing, and again . . . nothing, not even a wheeze. I went back to work on the main outboard. Jude was at the controls as I tried to coax it into life. It fired up momentarily and died again. The wind was picking up and I had to yell to be heard. I was yelling at Jude to push the starter but she couldn't hear me. I yelled again and again, a little louder each time, but still she couldn't hear. By the time I'd reached full pitch, all the people on board the many boats moored around us could hear me. It's quite amazing how far sound travels over the water with wind in its favour. The number of onlookers was phenomenal, all watching the drama and listening to me screaming at Jude. I cringed when I realised these were all our new neighbours. There was no way that motor was going to start again. Luckily, there were two young boys playing in a very small rowboat over by the shore. I hailed them and they kindly rowed out and ferried my family, one by one, to safety. After about an hour it was my turn to jump ship. When we arrived back at the house I stood on the deck overlooking the bay with the telephone in my hand. Down on the water was a very sad-looking, bright-orange cruiser with . . . oh my God . . . . still emblazoned down the side as clear as day, *MY DINGALING*. I called the boat yard and told them where they could collect their boat.

The following day, I watched *MY DINGALING* get towed away and I went back to the boat yard undaunted. I spotted a new 2100s Signature in the showroom, a very fast ski boat called *Captain Blackbeard*, and what a wonderful boat it was. I towed it home and the following weekend I put Jude and Mum and Chris onto the ferry to Rottnest Island while Greg Paul ('GP', who is one of my best mates), together with some of the crew and cast, set off in *Captain Blackbeard*. This name was apt, since I was sporting long hair and a beard at the time. We beat the ferry and ran up on the beach outside the local pub. We collected my family from the wharf and settled in for a great day at the beach, taking rides in the boat, launching easily right off the beach. Cruising over water that was such a beautiful clear aqua, we could see manta rays sailing through the water and dolphins playing on the surface. This was paradise. At around 2 p.m. a boat race started from the jetty and we decided to follow it around the island. I figured that Jude and Chris would be safe to join us as the water was dead calm, like a millpond. The bigger boats took off very quickly, and though we may well have been able to stay with them, I carefully stayed out of their wash, closer to shore, and we just cruised.

On the far side of Rottnest, while doing around 40 knots, I saw a massive shadow under the water out of the corner of my eye. I watched as this living missile moved towards us at great speed, on a collision course with our boat. Not wanting to raise a panic I said nothing and just kept driving.

Above: Pure decadence — 'The Boats'. In front, *Blackbeard,* 2100s Signature; behind, *Phantasea* 34-ft Diavolo.

Right: Me push-starting boat — I jest.

Suddenly a huge black fin broke the surface off our starboard beam. It was immense, quite terrifying, then just as quickly it went back down and under the boat. No one said a word. Judging by its shadow and fin, it was much bigger than my 21-ft boat! Needless to say, we headed straight back to the beach, where we spent the next couple of hours retelling our adventure tale to anyone who would listen. The locals we spoke to, back at work on Monday, all seemed to think from our description of the fin that we had seen a Great White shark. On the trip home, with Jude and family safely on the ferry, we followed closely in its wake. By now the Fremantle Doctor (the regular afternoon wind) had come up and the safest and most comfortable ride back was in the big boat's wake. That nice, safe position though, quickly became boring. I was tired of playing follow the leader and so I started weaving behind the ferry and jumping the swells. Delighting in the growing hysteria of my passengers, I had no idea that the ferry staff had turned its on-board video camera on us and everyone on board was being entertained by the antics of *Captain Blackbeard* and his 'crew'. I do know that Jude was one passenger not watching the screen. She tried not to let us out of her sight as we sank behind huge waves and then exploded into the air, at times 10 or 12 feet above the water, the hull and propeller completely airborne. And they tell me I'm a thrill-seeker! As the photos will prove, we managed to get home safely, despite some of us having to respond to nature's call out in the middle of the ocean. Once again, we were told later, we had been fooling around in shark-infested waters. I guess it could have been worse . . . we could have done a little water-skiing.

Three months of wonderful weather followed, with most of the same gang accompanying me on *Blackbeard* many times — maybe they were as crazy as me. We all had a fantastic time in Perth, capped nicely by a sell-out season, but then it was time to move the monster (the show) to Adelaide. We were to close the show on a Saturday night and Christmas Day was the following Tuesday.

Signpost on the Nullabor somewhere between Perth and Adelaide.

I decided to drive across the Nullabor in my Prelude and ship the Falcon and the boat on transporters. Rather than make the family endure the very long journey, they flew to Adelaide on Christmas Eve. I had been given a few solid tips on long-haul travel from the locals and I took careful note. I even put mesh over the intake for the radiator so that bugs wouldn't cause the car to overheat. They had also warned me to watch out for kangaroos. Really? Kangaroos? I departed on that Sunday with a very full car, including the family's Christmas presents. I had it figured I would arrive, like Santa Claus, on Christmas Day. What WAS I thinking? This was a VERY long way, especially on your own, and it was extremely hot and dusty. There I was, heading across totally unfamiliar country, with very little idea of where I was going, to find a house that I'd never seen before. I had organised for Andrew Pain, our company manager, to venture ahead and find a suitable property for me to lease for my family. He had found a place near the water, he assured me, and we arranged for the family to be collected from the airport and delivered to their mystery home.

Sunday was mostly without drama and I was making good time. As the sun began to sink and the odometer tripped over yet another hundred kilometres I felt fine and thought I could drive all night. I had no plans to stop yet, I had a goal and it was firmly in my sights. Then it happened: red, white and blue in the rear-vision mirror. I quickly checked my speed — no problem there, I had been in cruise control for ages. I pulled over and the officers approached my car.

'What have I done wrong?' I quizzed myself as they took a look at my licence. They then began to describe in vivid, gory detail, roos the size of small sheds leaping from the dark along this road and the wreckage that would be left of me and my car if I met one. They directed me to the next motel where they impressed on me that I should stay the night. I did . . . funny that.

The next morning, bright and early, around 6 a.m., I fuelled up and was on my way again. Even though it was broad daylight, as the kilometres clicked by I still watched out for Big Reds —

I needed something to help pass the time. The road is a dead-straight line and when cruise control keeps you at 100 kph you start to believe that you could get out and walk, though I strongly advise against it! I drove all day and was truly blown away by the sheer size of Australia. Late that evening I stopped for food and, mindful of the friendly traffic officers' words of wisdom, I grabbed a few hours' sleep. When I awoke it was Christmas Day and I was on the road at first light. I managed to reach Adelaide around midday and I figured this was not a bad effort considering the two stay-overs. I found what was to be our home for the next three months, in a place called West Lakes and it was ideal. Well done, Andrew, and many thanks.

It was great to see the family safe and sound and we were all there together on Christmas Day. All was well, except for one small thing — no turkey! Jude had arrived on a public holiday and there I was, on Christmas Day. Neither of us had given a thought to food in our move and, try as I might, I could not find anywhere to buy a turkey. Thankfully, we did manage to borrow a tree from some friendly neighbours who were going on holiday. I think Jude would still be angry with me today if we hadn't at least had a tree to put our gifts around. Chris, of course, had a great time anyway because we were all there with him and the presents had arrived safely.

This particular house had an indoor heated swimming pool, which was well used during our stay, and it was right on the man-made lake. Every day people could be seen wind-surfing and canoeing right in our back yard — fantastic. The boat and other car arrived in due course, as did all our tour boxes, including Chris' toys, making both us boys very happy. The boat was a little too large for the garage so we had to park it in the driveway, sticking out onto the pavement. No one complained, thank goodness, or I have no idea where we might have put it.

The show previewed and opened smoothly, and the reviews were glowing. The show was off to a great start, with solid bookings and the opening night party was, as usual, a knockout. There were ice sculptures everywhere and the world-renowned Cosette symbol took pride of place. It's quite amazing how the Cameron Mackintosh shows have always been instantly recognisable, even without a word. *Cats*, those amazing eyes; *The Phantom*, of course, the mask; *Les Miserables*, Cosette and the flag; *Miss Saigon*, the helicopter. These symbols are instantly recognised, worldwide, which is a truly remarkable marketing exercise. It's not hard to understand why the Cameron Mackintosh people have become so successful and why I'm delighted to have worked with them for 11 years. I still get butterflies whenever I see images of the shows, which will always be such a huge part of my life. Whether I catch sight of the magic imagery on a billboard in the background of the 'Dave Letterman Show' set, or in an amateur production somewhere, the feeling is always the same.

Philip Quast, my old friend from the Sydney season of *Les Miserables*, had returned to play Javert for the Adelaide and Auckland run. Anyone who has experienced this man's work will understand how thrilled I was at his return. The rehearsal process had been wonderful — Gale Edwards has a magical touch, to say the least. Even though Philip had just finished playing Javert in the West End, with Gale's fresh approach we all rediscovered the piece together. An awesome experience.

Philip, in a past life, had been involved in commercial fishing. So, no sooner had I suggested that we should toss out a line some time than we were on our way. After a Saturday night show we all met at the marina. This particular evening Guesty (that would be me) and the crew: GP (Greg Paul), Gooch (Ian Blackburn) and Quasty (Philip), put up the bimini top on *Captain Blackbeard* and went out in search of snapper. Well, from the very moment we left the dock we were swooshing around between huge waves. This was a little tricky since it was pitch-black and we were in a 21-ft ski boat, not a nice deep-bellied fishing trawler — not necessarily the wisest move of my boating life. We ploughed through the darkness for about 20 minutes, all a little shocked at the size and ferocity

Charity concert, 'Morning Melodies' — with *Les Miserables* cast, 1990.

of the swell. Finally we all decided we had to turn back, but by this time, heaven only knows how, Gooch had managed to curl up on the floor between the two front seats and was sound asleep. As we turned the boat around and were momentarily side-on to the waves we wore a beauty; sometimes sailors call these rogues 'the seventh wave', the unexpected extra in a 'set' which is usually six waves. This giant had built out of nowhere and as it crashed in on us, tearing the covers clean off the boat, it managed to dump gallons of freezing seawater straight in on a snoring Gooch. Well . . . what a shocking way to be woken! I reckon the scream he let out is still echoing around South Australia.

After the initial shock we all burst into laughter, especially when we realised how stupid we must have looked, bobbing around in the sea in the middle of the night, soaked to the skin. Shivering violently as the chill settled into our bones, we made the windy and wet journey back to port. It seemed to take for ever, probably made worse at the time by our disappointment at not fishing, but whenever we felt the blues creeping in we just had to remember the sight of poor old Gooch and the look on his face as he scrambled to his feet. We all, however, learned a very good lesson: you should always check forecasted weather conditions before any boating adventure. Though I'm sure we weren't in any real danger then, I guess one never knows what the elements have in mind for you, and it is definitely best to be prepared. Everyone was shocked we arrived home so early — especially us!

We did manage another outing together on *Blackbeard* not long afterwards, where we did actually fish. I caught a Banjo shark, and before I could even finish saying, 'What's that?' Philip had cut off its tail for bait, and gutted it — all over the floor of my boat! We all had some fun, as we managed to get out on the water-skis as well. The waters weren't exactly flat though, and I had a bit of a struggle keeping the boat trimmed, so as not to jerk the tow-handle from Quasty's grip as he continued to jump from wave to wave. I still don't know how he managed to stay upright.

Jude was looking wonderful as she approached full term with our second child. We had enjoyed another blistering run in Adelaide and were soon to move to Brisbane. The company was working well together and we were all loving the show. Every now and then we used to put together what we called 'Morning Melodies'. This was a concert where the cast donated their time to perform, mainly for the elderly and people who couldn't get to an evening show, or in some cases couldn't afford it. Occasionally, our management also arranged transportation for people in hospital to attend. I usually ended up hosting the mornings, a real treat for me. They were always a big success with the crowds, as everyone took the chance to perform songs that weren't in their usual repertoire. Everyone had a great deal of fun. These mornings did not just happen without a lot of effort and it wasn't only the actors who gave. Once again our hard-working crew were fantastic — without them, of course, these concerts could not take place. The company's management orchestrated the events with a great deal of generosity of spirit, making it a wonderful combined effort. The admission was usually around $10 and when you consider that we would often attract about 2000 people, it would regularly amount to a healthy sum at the end of the morning. A little was retained for advertising and the balance went to charity. We all used to sit down together when the dust had settled and decide which charity or charities should benefit. In the past we had donated to a number of very worthy groups, including the Cancer Foundation, Rape Crisis centres and cystic fibrosis research. On one particular occasion, we wanted to divide the money between four charities, but were undecided for a few days on which they should be . . . .

The following day was a scorcher, with the temperature in the high 30s and I decided to take the family to the zoo. Let me say now, that animals in zoo cages have never been one of my favourite things. I believe that all animals should be allowed to live in their natural environments and not be incarcerated simply for humans to be able to gawk at them at their leisure. Having said this, I do accept that most of us would never see a lion or a tiger or an elephant in our lives, were it not for zoos. A no-win situation, I guess. If we must have the compromise that is a zoo, it must be a situation in which the animals are cared for and treated well, as a priority over and above the interests of the paying public. I feel exactly the same about using circus animals. There are some great zoos, such as the one in San Diego, in the United States. This is one of the best I've seen, where the animals are enclosed in areas that, as closely as possible, resemble their natural habitats. I also understand that many animals would now be extinct if it weren't for the work done in and by the zoos of the world.

So, we wandered about the zoo and Chris was really enjoying seeing all these fascinating animals close up for the first time. As the temperature rose steadily into the morning we saw a few animals enjoying, or at least coping with, the hot conditions. Lions and tigers, and some monkeys from the more tropical regions, were fine but the polar bears, sadly, were not. These magnificent creatures, used to sub-zero conditions, were displaying obvious signs of discomfort. They were pacing back and forth and as they made each turn at the ends of their enclosure they would hold out a limb in an attempt to cool themselves. Then, in frustration, they would throw back their heads and growl mournfully. These amazing beasts were desperate, and even their water was too warm so they had no way to cool down. I could not shake the image of those sad bears from my mind. When I arrived at work that night I decided to put the suggestion to the concert committee that we donate some of the funds to the zoo to buy a refrigeration unit for their polar bear enclosure. Thankfully the vote was unanimous. Management contacted the zoo and in due course the bears were treated to a cool pool. I was never more proud to be a member of that fine company of performers.

The Adelaide season flew by and Christopher seemed to have grown a little every time I stepped back into the house, as Jude grew ever closer to having our new baby. The Gulf War was in full flight and I recall how we were all so upset by distressing reports of the violence, brought to us every day by news programmes and newspaper headlines. It seemed to dominate everyone's thoughts and conversations. As a father, I recall feeling deep compassion for the families of those involved in that political game. We prayed that it would be over quickly and I guess the feelings we were experiencing were heightened by the emotion which drove the show we were performing daily. *Les Miserables* is a true testament to people fighting for what they believe in.

It was time to move the show to Brisbane. A few weeks before we finished in Adelaide, the principals of the cast flew to Brisbane for a press call. As part of the function, we were also asked to perform 'The People's Song' with the Queensland Premier. On landing in Brisbane, we were whisked off promptly in a fleet of limos to the Queensland Performing Arts Complex, where the media and various industry folk were gathered. Timing was crucial, as we were locked into a schedule from hell and we all had to be back in Adelaide for the show that night. Suzie Howie was, as always, travelling at a thousand miles an hour, doing what she does best — organising the multitude. *Les Miserables* provided my first chance to work with this dynamo and I'm delighted to say we've worked together many times since, and have become great friends. So, Suzie hustled us into the foyer, and at the appropriate moment the Premier moved onto the stage and announced us. We marched over to stand with him, each in our prescribed positions — me with the Premier on my left and the cast fanned out on each side of us. The Premier looked at me with fear in his eyes. We began to sing 'The People's Song', but sadly the Premier had been given the words to a verse we were not doing . . . oops! I wonder what did happen to the assistant who made this blunder. We covered well and everyone was very good-natured about it — at least in front of us.

Timing, it would seem, is always a big issue in my world. Two days before the Saturday night closing of *Les Miserables* in Adelaide, Jude went for a prenatal check and, while everything was just fine, the doctor confirmed she was on track to deliver our new baby on the following Monday. This was a challenge, to say the least. *Les Miserables* was previewing in a few days, so while I knew I had an obligation to be in Brisbane for the show, I was just as determined that I had to be with Jude for the birth of our baby. I had been there when Chris was born and I wanted with all my heart to be there this time. What were we going to do? Jude could have stayed in Adelaide and delivered the baby without me, but together we decided, thankfully, to make a dash for Brissie, with all fingers crossed. With the doctor's final assurance that mother and child would be OK, we organised our tickets . . . saying nothing to the airline (which may otherwise have had a fit!). We figured that what they didn't know wouldn't hurt them.

So on Tuesday, one day into 'overtime', the Guest entourage headed north. Can you imagine what it took for Jude to board that plane? Still, she didn't show any concern at all and we had had a last-minute checkup . . . all was fine. During the flight, which seemed to take forever, I found myself staring at Jude, waiting, silently, for the signal to 'go boil some water, bring me clean towels, and . . . yes . . . clear the plane'. Jude was wonderful, she kept looking at me, silently murmuring, 'It's going to be OK isn't it? You promised.' When the plane eventually landed, there was a very welcome limousine waiting. Our driver ferried us to the sanctuary of our new, temporary, apartment. In fact, it was two small apartments. Enough to accommodate us until the baby was born, when I planned to lease a house for the rest of the season. The driver was great, though he visibly aged when we mentioned that our baby was overdue. We giggled as he immediately slowed

The family — Jude, me, and our beautiful, darling baby daughter Amy (one day old) and Christopher.

the car. He gingerly applied the brakes, and avoided even the slightest dip in the road. He even warned us every time he needed to accelerate or turn a corner. His name was Dennis, and strangely enough, I was to meet him again many years later, when the family were much older.

The most beautiful baby girl by the name of Amy was born in the Royal Women's Hospital, Brisbane, on the following Friday. And I will be forever grateful that I was there to witness her arrival. We named our little angel Amy Patricia (after Jude's mum) Cosette, because it also seemed appropriate to include the name of my stage daughter in *Les Miserables*. She was beautiful, strong, already extremely vocal, and with a wonderful shock of glorious red hair. I bathed her, as I had Christopher, and spent a few wonderful moments with her . . . just Amy and me. Judy was just fine, and even though neither of our children had entered the world without making their arrival well and truly known, she was beaming. We were both as proud as we could ever be to now have a healthy boy and girl. What more in life could anyone ask?

Unfortunately, I had to race from the hospital to the preview of *Les Miserables*. As I had missed the press call that afternoon, Suzie asked me to go back to the hospital for a newspaper photograph — a shot of me with Amy and Jude. A photo call I would have done with great pleasure, but as by then it was 6.30 p.m. and the show started at 7.30 p.m., it clearly wasn't possible. I'll never forget Suzie's reaction. 'Well if you can't be there we will lose the front page.' What about it being opening night in an hour? Love ya Suzie . . . We made page three the following day.

When I took Mum and Chris to meet the newest member of the family, Amy was even more beautiful than I remembered. Chris held her gently in his little arms as she stared, trustingly up at her big brother. People wonder often, I've heard, how a person can feel abundant love for a first child and then have the same boundless love for a second. Somehow the love I had for my family

Two huge Spanish mackerel, caught off Hayman Island . . . not bad huh!

grew broader, stronger and more proud than ever with the birth of Amy. There is never a question of sharing love, it just grows and grows. These two children are the lights of my life. The following Tuesday we picked up Jude and baby Amy and I moved my brood into the house I had leased in Brisbane. The only problem with the house was that it was not air-conditioned. Anyone who has spent the early months of the year in Queensland will tell you it gets unbelievably hot, with the humidity nearing 100 per cent most of the time. Jude had been through so much hot weather during her pregnancy in Perth and Adelaide, and now Brisbane. All the hot spots in all the hot months.

After a few days, the cars arrived in Brisbane, along with *Captain Blackbeard* — the boat delivered to one end of town and the cars to the other. Obviously I had to collect the Falcon before I could collect the boat, so a full day was wasted traipsing all over town gathering our belongings. Once home, we realised the boat was, again, too big for the garage, so we had to leave it in the front yard where it took up the whole yard, and a little more. I flinched and waited for the complaints to roll in. We were delighted to learn that none of our neighbours were at all concerned. The weather was fantastic and it wasn't long before we were out on the water once more.

Performing *Les Miserables* eight times each week took a lot out of us so our recovery day, Sunday, was precious. In those days we didn't do a show from Saturday night until Monday. Some of the cast relaxed by doing as little as physically possible on their day off, others spent their time tracking down the best places to eat and some went touring for the best places to see. We, the so-called Boys' Club, hit the seas, choosing to put our lives in the hands of Mother Nature and the elements. More often than not we would head off very early on a Sunday morning from the closest boat ramp. We fuelled the boat, loaded our kit with drinks, sandwiches and the best bacon and egg pie anywhere (thanks Jude) and launched *Blackbeard* with high expectations for a great day. Actually, taking into account the truck-loads of fishing tackle, rods, reels, bait, lures and so on it's a wonder that we didn't just sink. Still, the intrepid adventurers took life by the throat . . . and strangled it. Sorry, can't resist a little melodrama.

On one particular Sunday, with perfect weather and a great early start, we motored across the bay on our way to Fraser Island. Four of us, and all our gear — we figured the fish did not stand a chance. The Boys' Club at that point in time consisted of GP, Gooch, Dave Etheridge and yours truly. We had become hard-and-fast friends on this tour and our adventures had just begun. We felt like real fishermen, scanning the horizon for a sign of feeding birds or subtleties such as fish leaping from the water — always a giveaway — to pick the ideal

At the end of *The Phantom* we were presented with this poster showing dates and places we had all shared on this epic journey.

From left: me, Michael Cormick as Pharaoh, Marina Prior as Christine and Martin Croft as Raoul

Phantom company photo on the Masquerade stairs, Auckland 1997–98.

Above: A gift of a Phantom bear from a fan.
Right: Face-to-face with Sir Andrew Lloyd Webber, at publicity for the three Andrew Lloyd Webber shows, Melbourne State Theatre, 1992.
Below: Dressing Room One, Princess Theatre, Melbourne. Opening night of *The Phantom* and the beginning of my Phantom journey.

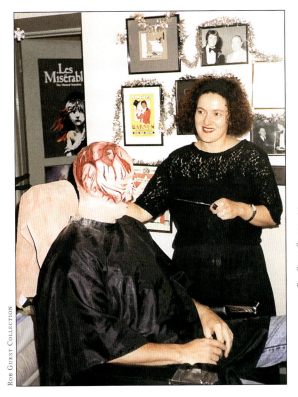

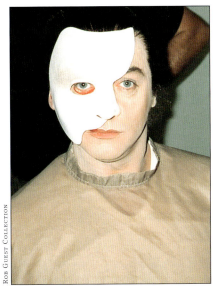

Left: My make-up artist Robina and a dozing Phantom — well it *was* a two hour process.

Above: The nearly-finished product.

Below: Make-up procedure almost complete on the Phantom. Gluing down the wig as stage management talk through technical details.

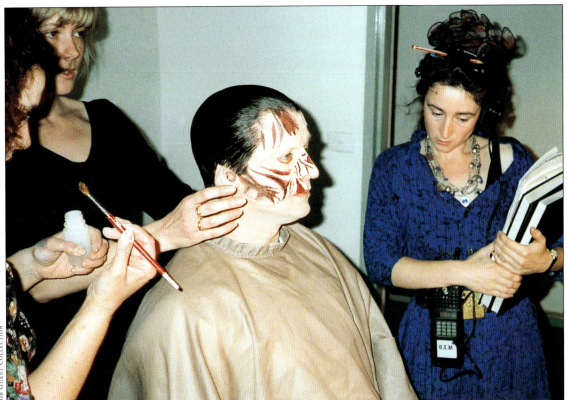

Behind the wheel of a Qantas jumbo — who's a petrol head now? This is the only time the Phantom left the building in make-up.

Above: Left to right: John Robertson, Marina Prior, me, Suzie Howie and Sir Cameron Mackintosh, at the press launch for *The Phantom* in Sydney.

Below: At home in Sydney . . . my 'red car' phase.

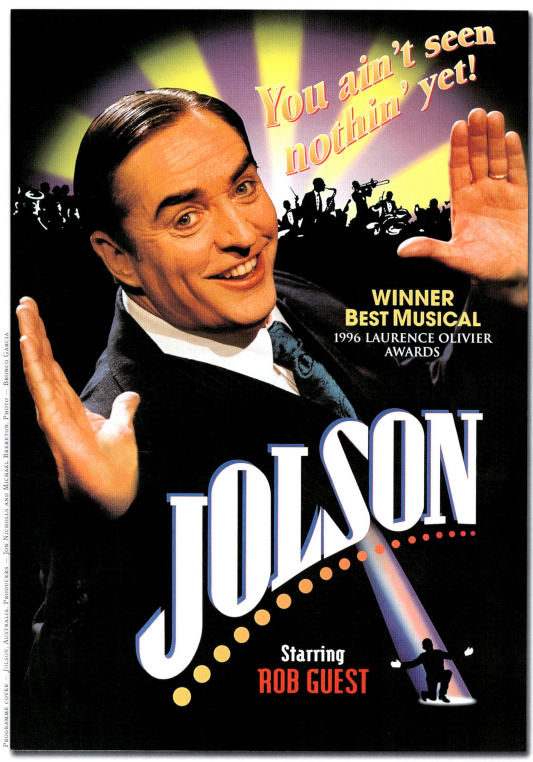

Programme cover for *Jolson* 2000/2001, Brisbane and Sydney. I always thought I looked like the Joker from *Batman* in this shot.

spot to drop our lines. Suddenly a flock of birds began swooping at the water just ahead of us. The feeding frenzy was amazing and the water was bubbling violently, so I cut the motor and we drifted towards the action. Lures were called for here. Four would-be fishermen fumbled with their lines in the very confined space of a ski boat. The odd profanity could be heard, not from me of course, as the sharp end of a lure found someone's fingertip, but while the boat rocked around under us, the first line was cast into the middle of the feeding school. BANG! A hit! The second line was on its way. BANG! . . . again. Two were reeling in as the other two cast their lines. We got into this crazy rhythm, casting and reeling, casting and reeling. We had stumbled across a school of Spanish mackerel and within minutes we had fish on the boat, in the air, on our laps, on our lines . . . everywhere. As quickly as it had all begun, it stopped. We looked at our catch, momentarily speechless, then threw back those we knew we couldn't eat. The tally was 16 fish, not counting the ones that got away.

The show was doing wonderful business, as it had everywhere, and we were very aware that Brisbane was the last centre on this tour of Australia. Then we would cross the Tasman to play the final season in Auckland. The danger in doing a long-running show is that boredom can set in. Not everyone, obviously, can have the satisfaction of playing a leading role, so many cast members (not necessarily in *Les Miserables*) find that they need an extra outlet for their creative talents. They need a chance to perform something other than the pieces they sing every night. Thus, over many years a tradition was formed: an event called the 'Pink Dingo'. On these evenings the whole company

With Gooch (Ian Blackburn) at a 'Pink Dingo' night in Brisbane.

gathers to perform, in cabaret, their choice of song, usually one they have always wanted to perform but have never had the chance. It is always a fabulous night where performers and friends gather for pure fun.

Brisbane's Pink Dingo was no exception. We took over a hotel, and when I say took over I mean it. We had it fully occupied, floors of rooms were filled with cast and families and we commandeered the ballroom. The hotel owner was extraordinarily helpful and generous in making this evening possible. We had decided on a big-band night and our orchestra members joined in with gusto. Musical charts were begged, borrowed, or stolen, tuxedos and ball-gowns were dusted off and pressed and hair slicked or coiffed. We had Amy and Christopher tucked safely away in a suite upstairs and Jude, Mum and I took turns checking on them. The evening was a blast and the songs of choice that night seemed to be all big-band swing numbers.

As the following Sunday approached, I decided that the fishing had been too much fun not to try for more, so off I went again planning a day on the water. A major obstacle loomed — no crew. Most of the Boys' Club had made other plans and only Gooch was free. Undeterred, the two of us decided to go alone. Very, very early on Sunday morning we set out. The weather was good and the seas were calm. It didn't take us long to find the spot where we had previously made the catch of the year. We waited, changed lures, tried baiting the lines. In fact, we tried everything short of dynamite without even as much as a nibble. All day we sat there pondering the fickle pastime which should be called fish-feeding. Though something kept removing our bait, we never felt a single tug on the line, so we had lunch, drank a couple of beers, told a few lies and laughed and laughed, and still there were no fish. We sat out there all afternoon, changing positions occasionally until the sun began to set. I wasn't too keen to head back in the dark, but as *Blackbeard* did have full navigation lights and a searchlight, I managed to convince myself we could always find our way home. Time, and daylight, passed while we were busy discussing the pros and cons of evening boating, and then around the island came a huge white passenger liner. As it closed in on us we saw that she was the *Royal Viking Star*. Suddenly Gooch unleashed a plan. We needn't follow markers all the way back to Brisbane in the dark, all we needed to do was follow in the wake of the liner and cruise home safely and comfortably. As the seas were starting to turn nasty and storm clouds had been gathering for an hour or so the plan seemed like a good one. As predicted, the liner's wake provided a place of tranquillity compared with the treacherous, dark and foreboding seas all around us . . . and the heavens opened. From our tiny craft we could clearly make out passengers sitting at tables having dinner in complete comfort and luxury. Well, to begin with, they were dry! The weather worsened, and although both Gooch and I were starting to experience real terror, neither was prepared to admit it. We had been behind the giant for about 30 minutes when I started to feel she was pulling away. I tried to keep up but her wake had become turbulent, so I had to back off and away from her propellers. She was moving away rapidly now, and though I would not have thought it possible, the rain was growing still heavier. Lightning was striking around us and the deep rattling rumble of thunder added to our less than buoyant mood. Gooch reached for the chart to see where we were but the fierce wind ripped it from his grasp and shredded it before our very eyes. We were now riding crests longer than the boat and when we reached the top and looked down over the bow it was like peering into a black abyss, bottomless. I was having trouble maintaining forward motion as the prop kept leaving the water. We broke out the flares, things were getting seriously ugly.

Now we were both standing, with our hands gripping the windscreen, braced against the elements as the sky continued to throw everything it had at us. Then, we heard it. Faint at first, but as the moments passed it grew to a roar that could freeze your heart. What was it? Gooch was desperately trying to piece the chart back together. The *Royal Viking Sun* was now a speck on the horizon, appearing and disappearing between swells, which had become mountains. We both started to think the worst. We were now screaming at each other, as the time for self-control and politeness had well and truly passed and the roar grew louder and louder. We had not the faintest idea where we were and the sky and sea, through our stinging, bleary eyes, now blended into one. Was the shoreline on my port or starboard and what was that ever-growing roar?

Both of us argued about where we were until Gooch suddenly cried, 'Oh my God! It can't be!' 'WHAT?' I screamed.

Gooch yelled back, 'Quick, turn around!' As I did we were almost capsized by a rogue wave the size of a small city. 'WHAT?' I screamed again against the wind.

'That noise,' he said, 'I know what it is! It's the surf crashing on Bribie Island!'

Was it possible? If so, we were 40 km off-course, heading towards treacherous, breaking surf in an open ski boat. We were about to be smashed to kindling.

God smiled on two miserable mariners that evening from hell. Out of the dark loomed a channel marker. If we were where we feared, there would be another soon, and sure enough there it was. By this time my hands, arms, legs, everything was in pain. Pain unlike any I had ever felt, and we were still being pounded. Through the night we ploughed on, one channel marker at a time, back to where we had been fishing hours before. Finally, we found the main channel and headed for the boat ramp. It was 1.30 a.m. in the morning before we got the boat back on its trailer and began the drive home. We were exhausted, sore all over and famished, but grateful to be alive. I learned another great lesson that day: never turn your back on the sea and never, ever listen to Gooch! Way too tired to clean the boat, I crashed, vowing to do the mopping-up in the morning. When I saw the mess she was in, in the light of the next day, the whole night's adventure came rushing back. I connected the hose to the motor, fired her up and went inside for a quick coffee. I had just stepped inside the house when . . . splutter, splutter, the engine stopped. *Captain Blackbeard* had just run out of petrol. I could not move! God had certainly been watching over us that night. Oh, yes . . . the *Royal Viking Star*? She was voyaging to Cairns, not Brisbane! Thanks, Goochey!

The remaining time with *Les Miserables* in Brisbane flew by. Amy and Chris grew every day and, before we knew it, we were getting ready to close and head to Auckland — the last stop on this amazing tour and the beginning of the end of the *Les Miserables* run. Dave, my brother, and Jenny, his wife, found accommodation for us in Auckland. Once again we were to arrive somewhere without knowing where we were going to stay. I remember, vividly, arriving back in New Zealand, and what a proud moment it was for me. I was coming home and bringing with me the gift of a truly wonderful musical. Suzie had, yet again, exceeded everyone's hopes and expectations — the terminal was full of media. As a result though, it took for ever to get through to Dave and the family. Another magic moment followed, a lovely reunion and Dave and Jen had found the perfect house for us. It was close enough to the Aotea Centre, where I'd be working, yet not in the CBD.

The lead-up to our first preview was a hectic time, as usual, trying to fulfil publicity commitments as well as rehearsing the show. The crew had done their customary magnificent job and everything was on schedule, despite the incredible amount of detail and red tape. Every single piece of equipment had to be labelled before transit, and we are talking about pallet upon pallet of staging equipment, sound, lighting, costumes and set. Each piece had to have a 'carnet' number for Customs. They insist that every single item brought into the country must be accounted for and guaranteed to leave the country when the show finishes. The logistics are daunting, but no one could have done it better than this fantastic crew. As usual, we were able to walk onto the stage at the Aotea and the set was perfect — it all looked and smelled just as it had in Brisbane a few short days ago. The only difference was that the auditorium and backstage of course had their own unique layout and feel.

People have often asked me what it was like on opening night in Auckland. For me the only word to describe that evening is 'magical'. My home town, that fabulous show and the audience loving it — I was so proud. The entire Australian production there in New Zealand and, although being the only Kiwi made for added pressure, I relished it! I was never allowed to forget that I'm a Kiwi. Every time the All Blacks played Australia, there was a standing $50 bet, whether I wanted it or not. At that particular time my wallet was taking quite a hammering because the All Blacks were also taking a hammering. The show received rave reviews and after opening night I received many phone calls, mostly from friends offering congratulations, but some from people I hadn't heard from in ages. One notable call came from my good friend Carl Doy. He said that a friend of his, Murray Thom, had seen the show and was wondering if I might be interested in meeting him, with a view to a new project.

We met at what was then the Regent Hotel, now the Stamford Plaza. This hotel has become very significant to me as I've had many fruitful meetings there since. Murray was wonderful and we immediately struck up a friendship which has grown steadily over the years, to the point where he is now one of my dearest and most respected friends. Anyone who knows Murray also knows that he has a wonderful knack for putting the right people together to make a project work perfectly. He also, most certainly, has an iron will. He not only knows exactly what he wants, he always gets it. The word 'no' simply doesn't register with him, and if he hears it at all it's like a red rag to a bull.

We agreed, in a very short time, to record a theatre album with Carl as producer, musical director and pianist. The problem we had was time — we needed to get into the studio as soon as possible to connect to the success of *Les Miserables*. Carl and I began the arduous task of selecting the songs straight away, which meant many difficult decisions because of the dozens and dozens of songs I would have loved to include. We were limited naturally by the length of recording time available on the CD, but certain tracks just had to be there. My first essential was 'Bring Him Home', and we also decided early on to ask the *Les Miserables* cast to perform 'Do You Hear The People Sing'. John Ockwell, a wonderful bass player, the show's musical director since Brisbane and a good friend, helped put this track together brilliantly. The list slowly started to make sense and Carl started on the musical arrangements. We were booked into Mandrill Studios, but given that I was doing the show every night with matinees on Wednesdays and Saturdays, our recording time was fairly restricted. We really only had 9 to 5, four days a week and this was going to be an amazingly busy time. Carl worked wonders in such a short time — the tracks were sounding great and I was itching to get started. Some of the songs were new to my repertoire and others were like old friends, the trick being to make them all sound as if I had just discovered them. The track listing called for me to use all the colours in my range, from belting top Cs in 'Pity the Child' to floating on my falsetto for 'Bring Him Home'.

I was loving the show in Auckland and the audiences were superbly receptive. We were sold out, everything was going splendidly. I began recording and even though my workload was immense, I was having a ball. I used to take the rough mixes of each day's work home so my biggest critics, who also happen to be my greatest fans, could make their critique. I did re-record a couple of vocals after I'd had a chance to listen to them a few times. I've realised over the years that there is no point in trying to be totally satisfied with a recording. Every breath in the wrong place, any wrongly placed note will haunt you if you let it. It could drive you insane. In general, it is a lot safer for the artist's mental health to leave the finessing to the producer.

Les Miserables had about three weeks to run and I was beginning to wonder what the future might hold beyond the show, which had been a major part of my life for three years. I was at home and Jude and I were having a coffee and fixing the problems of the world when the phone rang. It was the *Les Miserables* executive producer, and my very good friend, John Robertson. He came straight to the point: Anthony Warlow was leaving *The Phantom of the Opera* and Cameron wanted to know if I was interested in taking over the role of the Phantom. My world stood still. It took exactly a second to take a quick breath and say yes, while trying to stop my heart beating out of my chest.

I was to complete the run of *Les Miserables* and then have a short break before starting rehearsals — vocals first, with the amazing Brian Stacey. I was going to have to change my vocal style from the 'attack' I used for Valjean, to a more gentle, lyrical style, to facilitate the vowels and elongated notes and phrases of the Phantom.

First, though, was the album and the completion of *Les Miserables*, a full enough schedule to think about for the moment. I returned to the studio on the following Monday and buried myself in the task at hand. We were doing wonderfully, and everything was on time. On the Wednesday, the announcement was made, both in Australia and to the *Les Miserables* cast, that I was to become the new Phantom. My cast and crew, orchestra and friends were all so supportive it really made me proud to be a part of such a great bunch of people.

Arriving at the studio for a regular Friday recording session, disaster struck when I found that part of my voice just wasn't there. I calmed myself and decided to warm up for a little longer, try to coax it along. It would not respond, in fact it just seemed to get worse the more I tried. Eventually I had to call off the day's session. Usually when something like this happens during a recording I simply stop and rest, but of course I had the show to deal with that night. Quickly, I made a call to Dr Paul Simcock, who had previously removed my tonsils and is the best ear, nose and throat specialist I know. He saw me straight away and hit me with the bad news: I had a swollen vocal cord and he told me not to talk for a week. Not just 'Don't sing' but 'Don't make a sound'. I called the show's managers and broke the news that I was going to be off. Once again, they were great about it even though very concerned.

I've never been very good at being sick, in fact I think I'd have to be the worst patient anyone could imagine. It's not that I'm demanding, it's just that . . . well, I don't want to be sick and as much as people try to help me, I find it difficult to just lie down and accept it. In this case I probably wasn't as much of a pain to my family as usual, because I couldn't complain. I went to see Dr Simcock daily while recovering and he gave me cortisone shots in the hope that this would reduce the swelling.

The following Sunday the company was having 'The Hugo Awards', obviously named in honour of Victor Hugo, who wrote *Les Miserables*. It was an annual ceremony during which everyone got a roasting for any mistake they had made, on or off the stage. These nights were fantastic in bringing the company together, but to say that I was not in a party mood on that particular occasion would be an understatement. I felt as though the bottom had fallen out of my world and I really didn't want to be surrounded by my fellow performers and crew. Seeing them all having a great time, I was sure, would only serve to remind me how much I missed the show. You have to understand that a vocal problem like this is a singer's worst nightmare. It's not only your livelihood that's in jeopardy, but a situation like this can compromise your very essence, your sense of self-worth. There have been many instances where singers have never sung again . . . but I was not going to become paranoid.

We arrived at the nightclub for the awards, and from the outset everyone was so lovely. While they were positively thrilled that I could not talk, they were very sympathetic because it was a vocal problem. In situations like that everyone can see themselves in the same boat. Yes, I was well and truly roasted — I guess they couldn't resist the chance while I couldn't retaliate! Even my very good friend Dave Etheridge gave me hell. He accepted an award and proceeded to thank me for his shoes and his shirt and his tie, even his suit. Apparently they'd all been financed by winnings he'd collected from me during the tour, when I had backed the All Blacks against Australia. Everyone had a good laugh, including me, though my laugh was still silent. I don't remember what particular award they gave me, but I do remember that I made my way to the stage, determined to say thank you at least. Having not spoken at all for a few days, all I could manage was a whisper and no sooner had I opened my mouth than I was told to shut up, in the nicest possible way. Everyone understood that for me to get back in form for the show I needed complete vocal rest.

As I mentioned earlier, I had had to leave New Zealand in a rush to take up my position with *Les Misérables*. As a result I had tossed all my worldly possessions into storage. In my haste I'd opted to use a car container at a storage facility close to where I was living in Auckland. It had always been my intention to have it shipped to Australia when I was ready. I called the company, or I should say Jude called them for me, as I couldn't speak, and they said that the business had been sold while we were away and the container had been transferred to another suburb. I headed there immediately to check it over and collect a few precious pieces. When I found it alongside dozens of other containers, sitting out in the elements, I began to open it with mild panic. Once I saw inside, I was speechless with shock. The entire contents were soaking wet and mouldy and everything stank. It seemed that condensation had been forming on the inside of the roof and had been raining down onto everything for months. I could have cried, nothing was salvageable, but I couldn't say anything. All my show posters, stage suits, everything was ruined. I simply closed the door and wrote a message for the yard owners to dump the lot.

By Tuesday, having not spoken for nearly five days, I decided it was time to try my voice again. Acutely aware that the show was closing on the following Saturday, I was determined to be back in form. I called John Ockwell to the theatre and we quietly ran a few segments of the show. My voice seemed reasonable. I didn't use any power but it seemed clear, so we took it a little further by testing my falsetto — it was OK, though still not perfect. I figured that was understandable since I had not used my voice, at all, for so long, so I attempted the soliloquy. There it was — a devastating gap in my vocal register.

I tried to warm it up and managed to regain a little more voice. John was being incredibly supportive, and I have to say this problem came as a shock to everyone, not just to me. I had always been known as 'iron chords'; nothing stopped me, until now.

Frustrated and more than a little anxious, I mulled over my medical situation and hummed gently all the way home. When I told Jude the outcome I could see she was disappointed for me and I was beginning to feel pretty low again. I decided the only thing to do was to tackle the problem head on. I told myself, firmly, that I did have enough voice to do the job and I rang the theatre to tell them I was coming back . . . TONIGHT. They were overjoyed. Mid-afternoon I had a nap, then showered and went to the theatre a lot earlier than usual to get my mind back on track and to check out a few things. My mind was playing games — had I made the right decision?

Could I really do this? It was show time and everything seemed strange as I had never been away from the show for that length of time before. It was great to be back, even if it was absolutely terrifying.

The show opening was fine, if just a little edgy. I was being careful, as careful as one could be playing the powerful Valjean. Then the true test came up, the soliloquy. Although I couldn't say it was perfect, it felt OK. I was back, getting stronger and it felt wonderful. Then it happened — suddenly. My voice just gave up without warning. You could have parked a car in the gap in my register; and we were only halfway through the first act. I knew I was in real trouble. I struggled with most of the 'big' singing through until Act I was done, then I knew I had nothing at all left for Act II. At that point I had to tell stage management that I was going to go off before Act II, rather than subject the paying public to what I believe would have been a disaster. To do this was the hardest thing I have ever had to do — admit defeat — even though I knew I had no choice.

In solemn silence, I made my way home. I just couldn't believe it. Never in all my years performing had my voice ever let me down to this extent. I was crushed. Neither had I realised until then just how much I took my voice for granted. The next day the telephone rang off the hook. Everyone wanted to know what had happened, including the media. I didn't feel ready to deal with the inquisition, so I was glad I could hide behind my lack of voice. Jude was able and, thankfully, willing to step in to fend off the callers' questions. I scribbled notes for her and she covered for me beautifully. Everyone was very good about it, and I went back to see Dr Simcock who told me that, while I had been a very naughty boy, luckily I hadn't done any more damage.

The next week dragged like a month of wet Sundays. Finally, Friday morning rolled around and I figured it was time to try again. I warmed up gently and I steamed my throat. In fact, I did everything known to modern man to prepare my voice for song. I WAS going back — that night. So the pressure was really on . . . would it happen again? Could I get through it? It wasn't the best vocal I had ever delivered but I made it. Yes, I managed to get through the whole show. The following day was Saturday and that meant two shows and the second show was to be the very last for the *Les Miserables* run. I decided not to do the matinee, so that I would be at full strength for the final show, or as good as I could be under the circumstances. I made it! Tears were shed by the bucket-load as we came to the end of this wonderful, emotional journey.

8.
The Phantom

EVEN THOUGH I KNEW I was going on to do the *The Phantom*, I was sick at the thought of leaving *Les Miserables*. It had been such a huge part of my life for so very long. I could not possibly have known that the fates would bring us together again in the future. Sadly, we bid a fond farewell to all our friends in the cast, crew and orchestra and we set about the daunting task of packing up the show. Our plan was to spend a few days in Dunedin with the family and then fly back to Australia. I decided to go back earlier than the family because we needed to find a place to live, this time in Melbourne. I was beginning to feel as though we'd been touring forever.

While staying with Andrew Pain I found a house to lease in the suburb of Sandringham and managed to have the furniture delivered from storage just before the family arrived. Ah, timing again! The next step was to retrieve the cars from Brisbane. I flew up, traded the old Falcon for a 4WD, coupled up the boat and drove back to Melbourne. Rehearsals gave me a good chance to stretch the vocal chords and I was delighted to find that my voice was completely back to normal. Brian Stacey worked with me for about a week, just gently changing my vocal style from *Les Miserables* to *The Phantom*.

The album was on hold, so I flew back to Auckland for a week to make a few timely amendments to the tracks we'd already completed. Walking back into Mandrill Studios momentarily brought back all the insecurities I'd experienced when I had no voice. Thankfully, I was back with full strength now, back with a vengeance. Feeling terrific, I managed to fix vocals that I hadn't been happy with and scoot back to Melbourne in plenty of time to start 'blocking' the show.

Joanne Robertson was the resident director and her insight into the Phantom made my life much, much easier. This character is deceptive. At first the part seems very simple, but the more you study him, the more levels you discover to the persona. It is this depth and the constant and fascinating process of uncovering new layers that kept me keen to play the role for so long. Bob McCarron was responsible for designing the prosthetics for me. He is one of the best make-up artists in the world. His many credits in film stretch from *Dead Calm* with Nicole Kidman, Sam Neill and Billy Zane

Opposite page: The Phantom at the organ — from the programme; also used as publicity shot.

In my dressing room, dressed and ready to head for the stage. I *never* sat down in this suit.

to the 'high-tech' likes of *The Matrix* with Keanu Reeves. We became firm friends and I thank him sincerely for creating a look that was purely MY Phantom. During this time I really had my work well and truly cut out for me, what with rehearsals, publicity and vocal training. I was having a ball.

The Phantom is a very insular character, both on stage and off. In the early days of the production, I would arrive at the theatre to begin the make-up process two full hours before my fellow cast members and leave the theatre, at times, almost an hour after they had gone home. I often felt the profound isolation of the Phantom was my own, and this made it very difficult, sometimes, to touch base with people.

As the opening night approached, everything doubled in intensity. At times like that you can very easily begin to feel like a product rather than a person: standing endlessly for costume fittings, make-up sessions every day and pacing about in the costume to get the feel and flow of the garments. Once all this was set, it was time to bring the character to life, to deliver this wonderful story, to be truly believable and sing with full heart and commitment to the role. This was a challenge behind the mask, as it obscured more than half my face. I had to find other ways of expressing myself as the character.

Opening night finally arrived with much fanfare and nervous tension. It is a day that I will always remember, that day in December 1991. My dressing room looked like a florist shop and Norman had outdone himself organising my personal things to make me feel at home. I had a video and TV, which was tuned in to the closed-circuit camera focused on the show, so that I was always aware of what was going on, on stage. I had a microwave oven, pot plants and framed photos everywhere. The largest object in the room, however, was a fabulously comfortable barber's chair, in which I spent many, many hours . . . no, days. There were three of us in this room, my 'lair' if you like. Norman worked on the details of the costume, Robina's job at that time was to apply the prosthetics (no mean feat), and we became like the three musketeers.

So, the moment of truth had arrived. It was time to draw on all that had been extracted from me by the talented director, time to use all that careful guidance and call on everything I had been taught. It was time to launch my Phantom onto the stage for the first time. This must be the hardest moment for a director, as from that moment, really, there is nothing they can do but sit back and let someone else complete and deliver their work.

Marina Prior was, as ever, incredibly supportive, as was Dale Burridge, who played Raoul. Virtually the only direct contact that the Phantom has with anyone on stage is with Christine and Raoul. The only exception is a moment at the top of Act II, when the Phantom enters as Red Death.

The support from these two characters was therefore vital. The show opened without a hitch and as we headed into the 'First Lair' everything was on track; transition to the boat ride, seamless. I helped Marina from the boat and moved into 'Music of the Night' with no problem. Then came the mirror 'reveal' scene, in which Christine discovers the mannequin of herself that the Phantom has hidden.

At the prescribed musical moment, the mannequin, resplendent in a wedding gown, leans forward, causing Christine to faint. At this point, the script calls for the Phantom to move over to the boat and collect his cape to drape over the stunned Christine. Well, not on this night! A combination of new shoes and a glossy, newly painted stage floor (dewy wet because of the dry-ice mist billowing about the set) caused my left foot to whip out from under me. The Phantom fell. I hit the deck with my left hand and pushed myself back up onto my feet so fast that my backside barely touched the stage. I was OK and luckily, because of the mist, no one (I hoped) noticed. The rest of the show went according to plan and, as people came back to see me afterwards, Suzie Howie grabbed me to congratulate me. She asked if I was happy and we

JEFF BUSBY

Me doing something most people only dream of — keeping Suzie Howie quiet. Only kidding. I wouldn't be where I am without her.

agreed that, for a first night, it had gone well and while there were still a few things to fix, that would always be the case. I couldn't resist asking if she noticed my fall. She laughed and said, 'Of course, and so did the other 1400 people!'

The press were very nice and so my stint as the masked genius had begun. When Matt Dalco took me to lunch and said that they believed that *The Phantom of the Opera* would have a life of around eight years in Australia and New Zealand, I laughed. Not that I didn't believe it but . . . WOW . . . eight years. My contract was for a year. I adored the show and we were sold out a year in advance, which in this very fickle industry gave everyone a sense of security. Still, we never rested on our laurels. There was always a need for publicity. When a show becomes as big and as popular as *The Phantom*, it generates problems peculiar to itself. One challenge for the PR team was that the public were becoming frustrated that they could not purchase tickets. As the show was so well sold, people began to believe they would never get tickets, and so in some cases they just stopped trying. The management had to keep in touch with the public and constantly remind them that tickets to more performances were becoming available. After six months in Melbourne the Guest family decided to really settle down. We purchased a house in Hampton, the suburb adjacent to the one we were living in — in fact we practically moved just one street along. We were going to have to renovate, but it was perfect.

As the show continued, so did life away from the theatre — at quite a pace, but packed with fun.

THE PHANTOM 99

I changed cars a few times and bought a 34-ft cruiser, a Diavolo, which I named *Phantasea*. This boat was to become fairly well known around Saint Kilda marina and out on the bay. I took it out for one of the very first 'Great Outdoors' television shows, and had loads of fun showing the viewing audience the seals in the bay close up as well as some of the great restaurants at Williamstown. With my love of the water I took the chance to escape to the briny whenever I could.

And some of the best entertainment you could ever imagine occurs dockside. Moored in the boat pen, one can watch pure slapstick and, sometimes, high drama unfold. People take out those huge boats, have a great day, eat and drink way too much, and often discover on their return to dock that the boat has grown or the berth has shrunk. Their boat simply no longer fits — or so it seems. Add to this a bit of a breeze and a comedy of errors unfolds. I have seen captains throw their arms in the air in frustration, yelling abuse at anyone in their line of sight. Often someone is then ordered to take a dinghy out to pass a line to shore and pull the unruly boat into its ill-fitting pen.

Around Saint Kilda marina, the locals tell the story of a certain airline pilot who purchased a 34-ft Sea Ray. On its maiden voyage he managed to hit three boats before he even reached clear water. He returned to dock and turned in his keys, never to captain a boat again — and this chap was an airline pilot! I can attest that it's not as easy as it looks, driving one of those beasts, mainly because they don't have a keel to steady them and when the wind comes up they tend to drift sideways. If you are unfortunate enough to have the added complication of twin stern drives, well, it can get very, very messy. Most captains leave their boats out of their berths until the wind abates, rather than risk taking out a couple of half-million-dollar yachts which may be quietly bobbing on their moorings. Accidents are just around the corner when you are boating.

One evening while we were docking, after a great day's boating — GP on the bow, rope in his hands, ready to tie her off — the wind suddenly picked up. I was trying to turn the boat but she started to slip sideways. I managed to compensate, but by this stage I was well past our berth and there was no room to turn a monster like *Phantasea* in such a small area. The throttles had been acting up for a while so, when I thought we had no forward propulsion, in fact one of the engines was still pushing forward at about three knots. This movement would have been nothing to worry about at sea, but we were moving ever closer to a huge stone sea-break wall and here it was a distinct worry. Greg yelled and, too late, he straddled the anchor and with his feet he tried to fend off our 34-ft missile. Just as one foot went down between the bow and the wall, I managed to throw her into reverse. That might have been an enormous tragedy and thank goodness he wasn't hurt. But it just goes to show how quickly disaster can strike. We finally got her tucked away safely, but we were more than just a little shaken.

Another rather shaking aspect to owning a boat like this is the cost. Mooring fees, maintenance, anti-fouling, new batteries and so on. At that time I still owned *Blackbeard* as well, but luckily it was up in the stackables at Saint Kilda marina, safe and sound. People (cynics, I reckon) say, the two happiest days a boat owner will ever know are the day they purchase their boat and the day they sell it! My bank manager is right when he says boats are a big, black hole into which you just throw money . . . yeah, but sometimes you just have to do it, eh?

It was during the early days of *The Phantom* that I met a young guy named David Dixon. At that time he was playing Joseph, in *Joseph and the Amazing Technicolor Dreamcoat*, and as such he was living a past life of my own. We just clicked and, because he is also a serious petrol-head, we ended up playing with boats and jet-skis together. One day he called me to say he'd heard of a

Opposite page: 'The Boys' Club' on *Phantasea*, doing a publicity shot that made the front page — cool!

Scarab for sale that he wanted to take a look at, and before I knew it I was heading down to Patterson Lakes to check it out with him. He bought it and I don't think his wife, Belinda, will ever talk to me again.

It was at about this time that Sir Andrew Lloyd Webber came to town. He organised the casts of *Joseph*, *The Phantom*, and *Aspects of Love* to get together one lunchtime for a photo call. Not bad PR — three shows, all written by Sir Andrew, all in the one place, and he'd flown the cast of *Aspects* from Sydney for the event. This seems incredible, until you think he made the same grand, generous gesture with the casts of seven of his shows playing in London simultaneously. This was a fantastic opportunity for everyone to get together, even if just for a photo call.

The show just kept packing 'em in, until one day someone noticed a whole row of empty seats. Some of the younger cast and crew members started running about saying, 'We're not full! What's happening?' Most of these youngsters were new to the industry and, this being their first show, they had never known anything but full houses. Welcome to the real world. Apparently we were still sold out, and no one need have panicked. It turned out that one large, hapless party had been involved in a bus accident on their way to the show and while no one, we believe, was injured, they obviously could not get there to fill those seats.

Of course, there's also the story of the matinee performance where a gentleman looked across an empty seat at a lady. He said to her, 'Isn't it amazing, the show is packed and yet this seat between us remains empty.' Rather indignantly the lady responds with, 'Oh, no . . . this seat is paid for. It was to be my husband's seat but he has passed away.' 'Oh, I'm so sorry to hear that,' said the man, 'but couldn't a friend or relative have taken the ticket?' 'Oh no!' said the lady, 'you see, they're all at the funeral!' I know, I know . . . I just couldn't resist throwing that one in. The ushers even kept a diary of funny comments made by patrons and some of them were hysterical. Like the time a patron was told while purchasing her tickets that the seat she had chosen was behind a pole. She said, 'That's amazing! How do you know what nationality they will be?'

In any show, every action on and off the stage must be synchronised. Everyone must be sympathetic to the needs of the performance, the image and atmosphere it's creating. Untimely noise backstage always presents a challenge on stage and it is not ideal to have an usher open a theatre door at an inappropriate moment. Drawing the performer's attention from the scene at hand could be disastrous. The phrase 'breathe with the show' is an essential that works for us all. Everyone involved in the production of a show must learn to listen and act with the rhythm of the show. They have to seek the right moment to undertake even the simplest task, or risk throwing the performer's balance and with it the performance.

Whenever people came backstage on a tour and saw how well the costumes and props were looked after, how everything had its place, they were always blown away. The truth is that the show could not have lasted as long as it did without that attention to detail. We all looked after our costumes with extreme care. For example, once I was dressed for each performance, I would never sit down. My suit was made of French silk and although it looked wonderful, it would crease with ridiculous ease. As my first entrance was behind the mirror where the lighting showed every wrinkle, I found it best to stay standing until it was all over. After all, it wouldn't do to have a wrinkly Phantom.

Often, I suspect, people don't realise that there are a team of people working tirelessly to cover all the details we take for granted. Those unsung heroes who pave the way for us to tell the stories

Opposite page: Sir Andrew Lloyd Webber and Yours Truly — Melbourne.

and bring the characters to life never seem to get the credit they deserve. Like an iceberg, what you see in the performance is just the very tip, while most of the leviathan is below the surface, or behind the scenes. My thanks goes to them.

The Melbourne season was amazing and I don't believe another show, at least in my lifetime, will ever do a run to packed houses there for quite so long. Of course, at that time I didn't know I was heading to Sydney next and just how long I would play there — also to consistently packed houses. We were, indeed, part of a wonderful phenomenon.

Management called upon me to fly to Sydney to participate in the advance bookings launch. In fact it became routine for me to help with these launches in each new city and this was always a task I took on with great pleasure. Primarily designed to show the travel trade and group booking regulars what the show looked like, it usually entailed two functions, one at midday and the other around 6 p.m. All the guests would receive champagne, chocolates, preferential seat allocations at the upcoming shows, and we'd show video footage of *The Phantom*. Then the members of the cast would be introduced, a few would speak to the gathering for a while and we'd sign autographs.

Those advance showings, even today, hold the record for bookings. People were waiting for *The Phantom* to arrive and the old saying, 'give the people what they want', was the maxim we had to agree with as the crowds just poured in. Cameron Mackintosh was there for the Sydney launch and I had just signed for my third year. I had signed with little persuasion as I was enjoying the show immensely, and I also knew that the very moment I decided I'd had enough there would be a queue as far as the eye could see, waiting to take my place. Marina had also agreed to open Sydney, but she was only prepared to stay for six months. At this time she had been doing the show for a year longer than me.

When the time finally came to move to Sydney we engaged an agent there to find us a home to lease. I flew up one Sunday night to spend a full Monday having a look, with her, at what was available. Toward the end of the day I was starting to feel a little anxious as we'd seen nothing suitable and I had a plane to catch and a show to do that night. The agent called her office and they said there was one more house to view. It was in Roseville and if I was up to it, we could inspect it immediately. I agreed to take a look, and while it was going to cost a little more than we'd planned to spend (don't they all?), it was perfect. I agreed to lease it but the owners were overseas and the agent was going to have to get back to me. All the way back on the plane I kept thinking, 'What if they don't agree? We'll be back to square one! Please, please, please . . . don't make me do all that searching again . . . ' That place was just so perfect. As soon as I landed I took a call from the agents. The house was ours for six months, so I hurried home to show Jude the video footage I'd taken of the place.

We decided to take a short holiday on Hayman Island while all our stuff was transported to Sydney. Now, if you have ever been to this idyllic spot you will know what I mean when I say it is heavenly. The only problem was that we only had six nights and I started to unwind on day five. It's hard when you are used to doing eight shows a week, which amount to very full days, and rather late nights, to suddenly stop. The body and mind just don't switch off that quickly. We had managed to rent out our house in Melbourne and everything seemed to be on track. All we had to do was find preschools and so on when we arrived. The island is so peaceful, and because you are not allowed to land there unless you are a guest (excuse the pun!), tourists are kept to a minimum. Before we knew it though, it was time to go to Sydney. If I'd known then how long it would be before I got another break I think I would have relaxed more. Or would I? The beautiful launch took us back to Hamilton Island, where we caught the plane and headed to our new home. Jude loved the house, it offered plenty of room, a pool, and a great yard for the kids to live in. We proceeded to settle in and the cars and boat arrived without drama. I received a call from the boat broker in Melbourne, with whom I'd left *Phantasea*, to say he had a buyer. It was with mixed emotions I accepted the news that it had sold. I was happy it had sold easily, but as a flood of memories swept over me I felt very sad that it had gone. Silly, really. In retrospect I believe I should have kept it and brought it to Sydney. *Phantasea* would have been a perfect boat for Sydney's magnificent harbour.

Rehearsals were going well at the Betty Pounder Studios and, even though we had all done many performances, it was still good to get back to basics and rediscover our characters. When you take away the costumes and sets and make-up, you are left with the performance, only supported by the talent. It is wonderful to see. During rehearsals the organ was an ironing board and the music-box monkey was a cardboard box — we really had to use our imaginations. Those are the times most heavy with opportunity, the times for experimenting with a moment that you have wanted to expound on or improve. With only technical people there to watch and help you, if it doesn't work then you have the luxury of being able to try something else. I personally love this process because a character never stops developing. The knack is to make it grow in the right direction and, as a performer, you can only do this with the help of well-trained eyes and ears, who can advise and encourage from the audience's perspective.

The producers had pulled out all the stops for the Sydney opening. You couldn't move in Sydney without seeing 'The Mask' somewhere — billboards, newspapers, metro lights at bus stops. They'd also saturated television and radio with the news that *The Phantom* was here. We had been previewing for almost a week and everything was just fantastic. Opening night finally arrived and *The Phantom* took over Sydney. It was pure magic and the advance bookings guaranteed our stay for a very long time.

The opening night party was held at the Sydney Town Hall and the place was, befittingly, decorated with thousands of long-stemmed red roses. The image of the Phantom's mask was projected onto the walls and all the opening night guests enjoyed an abundance of wonderful food and champagne. Limousines lined the streets and the air was filled with the buzz of excitement and the word that the show was a great success. Success was something, with that sensational show, we may easily have taken for granted, especially given its track record, but everyone involved in the production always went to great lengths to make sure complacency never slipped in. Everyone constantly strove to keep it fresh and energetic. The fabulous pipe organ in the Town Hall provided a bonus theatrical point to the evening. An organist, dressed as the Phantom, played some of the music from the show as we partied until the early hours and finally, very tired but exhilarated, we headed home.

The next show after an opening night needs all your energy as you don't have the same feverish adrenalin pumping through your veins as you did before the opening. This is when the real work begins. After the show reviews and notices and after everyone has had their say on everything from the music to the make-up, we all settle down to do what we love.

Then comes the part that separates the men from the boys — performing eight shows a week. Let me tell you that it's simply not possible to feel brilliant before every performance, but when you hit that stage, hear that music, feel that audience, something happens to you. Something that cannot be easily explained and can only be understood through the experience. You can be tired, sick with the flu, whatever . . . and as you take to the stage something miraculous happens — a phenomenon fondly known as 'Dr Footlights' sweeps away your lethargy and carries you along on a rush of adrenalin. It is truly eerie. I have even hurt myself during a performance and not noticed until the show is over and I'm back in my dressing room.

During *The Phantom*'s run in Sydney, another popular show, *Beauty and the Beast*, began its successful run in Melbourne. Bob McCarron, our make-up guru, also did the make-up for the Beast, played by Michael Cormick, and this proved to be a huge bonus for me. Sonia, who was now my make-up artist, had always found it necessary to carry around a pot of special glue with her make-up quick-fix kit and watch my prosthetics like a hawk from the wings. The glue we used to fix my prosthetic face was prone to weakening under the extreme heat of stage lighting and, while I could never see it, occasionally my natural hair would peep out at the back. Well, it happened that the Beast's prosthetics required fixing with a glue that would not only stay stuck when it had to but was quick to remove. I was thrilled when Bob brought it to *The Phantom*, as it meant that not only would I be spared the embarrassment of visible hair, my time in make-up removal was cut from a tedious hour down to just twenty minutes — bliss!

Social commitments abounded as the whole of Sydney became, it seemed, obsessed with *The Phantom*. One night, as I was about to start my make-up, the phone rang. It was company management. They told me I was to expect a visit from the Governor-General of Australia. They also told me that he wished to meet me alone.

We delayed the make-up and I welcomed the Governor-General to the Theatre Royal. He came right to the point of his visit. He had been instructed, by the Queen, to ask me if I would be willing to accept an OBE. — the Order of the British Empire. Would I accept? This incredible honour absolutely floored me. So much so, that I could not speak to respond. Regaining my composure, and my ability to speak, I agreed to accept the honour. Then I was instructed not to tell anyone until the announcement was made on New Year's Day — I remember this was October. Once the Governor-General departed, of course, everyone looked at me with questioning stares, as I tried to pretend that the Governor-General often popped in for a chat. I couldn't say anything, even though I was bursting with excitement and busting to tell someone — anyone. I think I floated through the show.

Being honoured like that brings on feelings that are very difficult to explain. It means recognition for what you are trying to accomplish, and certainly that is gratifying. It is overwhelming and humbling, but I believe the distinction and pride is felt, in equal measure, by your parents. Again, I found myself with a pain in my heart, wishing my father had been alive to share my moment. He would have been so proud. I know he is, and I know my dear Mum is proud of me too.

Quite out of the blue one day, my agent called to say that the Grundy organisation wanted to see me about possibly hosting a television series. I was aware that Grundys produced 'Sale of the Century' as well as most of the top game shows. The question uppermost in my mind was, 'Do I want to host a game show?' — should they ask me to, of course. They sent me some videotape of the German version of the show and although I didn't understand a word, I did get the idea. So, keeping an open mind I decided to meet them. I could not see how it was going to be possible to fit a weekly television series into my already overloaded schedule, but I kept reminding myself to

A quiet coffee at Southbank, Melbourne, during taping of 'Man O Man'.

keep that open mind. By the time I returned to the show that night I was still none the wiser about the game show, but as I was having my make-up applied the phone rang. 'Well,' said my agent, 'you've got the new show "Man O Man" and they are willing to shoot two episodes every second Monday.' Hesitation was creeping into his voice as he finally said, 'The only problem is they are taping it at Channel 7, in Melbourne, so you'll have to fly on the Sunday from Sydney.' After my own moment of hesitation myself, I took a deep breath and boldly agreed to do it.

I need to explain this show for anyone who didn't see it. They gathered a group of 10 guys for each show, and arranged for 150 women to judge them on a number of attributes. These guys were paraded and examined for their body, their dancing, singing or peculiar talent and, of course, their personality. Immediately after they were introduced, four of the men were pushed into a huge swimming pool by 10 beautiful models, at the behest of the women judges, leaving six nervous contestants to begin the process of elimination category by category. At the end of each round, another man took a swim until finally a winner was selected. The show's pilot went well, except for the fact that the 150 ladies in the audience had been given an abundant supply of champagne. It became immediately obvious that the combination of alcohol and this show was a recipe for trouble. Real trouble, and it was MY job to keep some semblance of control over the proceedings. I had my work well and truly cut out for me by the time we reached the swimwear section. Holding the show together proved to be a real challenge when the judges began to allow their hands to wander everywhere and the long-suffering crew had to battle to move over-enthusiastic ladies away from specific areas of the set that I was expected to 'throw' to. It was a joke. Miraculously, the finished product looked good and so six episodes were to be shot. It was decided to reshoot the pilot as episode one but to limit the amount of champagne so that more control of the audience would be possible. We were scheduled in the 6.30 p.m. time slot on a Saturday night, pitched right against 'Hey Hey, It's Saturday', which was on Channel 9.

Darryl Somers sent me a lovely note upon the airing of episode one. It read, 'Congratulations on your new show, shame about the time slot.' I was chuffed to receive it and I sent a thank-you back to him in which I also agreed that the timing was a pity. I didn't want to compete with a show that I loved and, in fact, I'd appeared on numerous times, each time a riot of laughs for me. Our first show rated through the roof as did the initial six shows, fter which I was asked to do another six.

People could not understand my logic in doing 'Man O Man', especially as I was so well known for playing the Phantom. Why would I put my reputation on the line? Well, a few years before, David Marriner, the owner of the Princess Theatre in Melbourne, had offered me some sage advice. He said I should be careful not to become the anonymous man behind the mask. 'Keep your ownidentity,' he added, and I thank him for his wise words. 'Man O Man' allowed me to do something different and show a side that most people didn't know I had. Plus, it opened the door to many more opportunities. I do love presenting — I don't know whether I will present a game show again, but I did enjoy it.

We had been talking for some time about selling our house in Melbourne and buying in Sydney. *The Phantom* looked as though it was going to run for ever. Jude spent weeks looking at dozens of homes and when something looked promising enough to her, she'd bring me in to take a look. Nothing seemed right until one Sunday when a real estate agent rang and said that he had found what he thought was just the place for us. It was to be auctioned in two weeks and he said he thought it was well worth a look, even though it was a little further out of town than we had intended to go.

This was my one day off and I really didn't want to go house-hunting again, so when we couldn't find the place I was unimpressed, to say the least. We searched for a while, in vain, until we realised that the street we were searching was divided into two sections by bush land. Just as we were about to give up and head home, we found it. We walked through the front door and instantly loved it. It was everything we wanted. To tell it simply, we put in an offer, told the agent to let the owner know that we would not be at the auction, and two days later the owner, who was a car dealer, came back with a counter-offer and we met halfway.

The house in Melbourne then had to be sold in our absence. To add another distraction to the excitement at that time, Jude and I had decided to get married. We had a whole bunch of planning to do. So, there was a wedding to organise, a house to sell, a somewhat crazy television show to host and eight demanding performances of *The Phantom* to perform each week. Piece o' cake! We planned to be married in the back garden of the house we were leasing. We invited family and friends from Australia and New Zealand. As the Guest list swelled with the names of folks we had sorely missed, we knew the get-together, which should have happened long before, was going to be a huge day. As things happen in this crazy world, the Melbourne auction took place on the day before our wedding. All day I was on the phone to the auctioneer preparing the deal that I prayed would go through. Remember, I had already agreed upon the Sydney property and bridging finance never sounds too good.

It was 1 p.m. and the auction was in full swing. We had people arriving from everywhere, many planning to camp at our place, though we hadn't a clue where we were going to put them. I received a call from the agent to say the bidding was slowing, we were close, but not close enough.

I wondered about whether to take the best bid or if we should hold off and perhaps readvertise and try again. I knew thousands may have been wasted in that little exercise, but it is always a gamble. Then out of the blue, a bidder offered us our price on the proviso that he could defer making the full deposit for 30 days. This meant that we would get the price we wanted, if it all went through. If not we would be left high and dry. The risk factor was enormous, but never being ones to run from a challenge, we decided to accept and keep everything crossed.

Our wedding ceremony the next day went without a hitch. It was a relaxed and happy day and everyone seemed to have a great time helping us celebrate. Luckily too, within seven days the deposit for the house was in place and we were settled with our new property within the prescribed time.

As I was still doing *The Phantom* I was only granted a short break for our honeymoon. I hadn't told Jude where we were going but she believed we were going down to the south coast. Luckily, I was able to keep my plans secret and maintain the mystery until the last moment. I had arranged for our driver to take us to the airport on the Monday morning to see one of our New Zealand friends off on our way to the secret location.

Ken Groves, who was at the time head of Qantas promotions and a good friend, helped no end, and it wasn't until we were seated in the lounge of the Qantas club that I told Jude we were going to Hawaii. Well, she nearly fainted. Then in the next breath, true to form, she panicked that she hadn't said goodbye to the children properly, as she thought we were only going away for a couple of days. Of course they knew. They were in on the secret with me. The following week went way too quickly and before we knew it we were on the plane back to Sydney. I had actually arranged for a 10-day break, but my understudy had become ill, so on the day I returned I got a phone call to ask if I would come back the next day. I did.

The Phantom roller-coaster continued with incredible momentum and Marina finally, sadly, decided to leave the show. Her role of Christine was immediately and seamlessly taken up by Marie Johnson, who had understudied the role for some time. I had met Marie during *Les Misérables*, and while Marie and Marina are quite different actresses, each brought something very special to the role. Marie turned out to be another simply wonderful Christine. Before we knew it, we were into year two in Sydney and many other shows had come and gone.

The 'Cam Mac' organisation asked me if I would like to play the Phantom in London and, of course, I agreed. Unfortunately, 'Man O Man' prevented me from actually being able to take up the role. Amazingly, another opportunity to portray the Phantom in London arose a little later, but the fellow who was playing the role at the time changed his mind about leaving and so, once again, it didn't happen. I was in no rush to leave the Australian production as everyone, including Cameron, had said many times that our production was as good as any other in the world. I have to say, having seen productions in New York and London, I was very, very proud of our show.

After completing 19 episodes, the programmers decided to give 'Man O Man' a break so that we could catch up with the shows that were already going to air. The powers that be then decided to bring us back at 6.30 p.m. on a Friday. To my mind, this confused the public and we were put in the awkward position of having to recapture an audience. We didn't enjoy the same success the second time around and it took a few weeks before our ratings began to rise. Then, once again, we were moved back to Saturday night, where we quickly discovered that 'Hey Hey' had revamped and their ratings were huge. After 32 episodes, 'Man O Man' was no more. While there have been discussions about a comeback, and in fact it was aired in New Zealand (even repeated at some ungodly hour in the morning), I think the show has had its day in the sun. However, having fronted this show, producers did see me differently. I hosted the Australian Fashion Awards with Sigrid Thornton, and a pilot which went to air live, called 'Missing Pieces', a problem-solving show which, sadly, didn't get off the ground. I suspect it was swept away because most of the Channel 7 hierarchy were changing at about this time and we all know a new broom sweeps clean.

One of the most enjoyable hosting jobs I have ever performed was Carols in the Domain, known then as The Pacific Power Carols in the Domain, also for Channel 7. I had the pleasure of hosting this for two years. What a fantastic sight it was. I watched a sea of people, some 125,000, sitting happily together on the grass, singing joyously and listening to Christmas carols. The spirit of these events is truly uplifting. Plus, of course, the audience extended to millions of television viewers across Australia, New Zealand and even further afield. I have been invited to host this event since, but other commitments have prevented me from participating. Hopefully I will be asked again, soon.

Performing a show such as *The Phantom* has enabled me to meet people from all walks of life and people from every occupation you could imagine. Music is definitely a universal language and its appeal is vast, and timeless. A great number of my friends have some connection with the music industry, naturally enough. Often though, I've met people in simple and sometimes strange circumstances, who have also become much-valued friends. One chap, who walked onto my property about seven years ago and has become one of my best mates, is Greg Smart. He's a Kiwi with a keen business mind and a personality to match, who's worked wonders with his businesses in Australia. Greg now owns, among other ventures, one of the best tile companies on Sydney's North Shore — Tilesmart.

Being a car nut, I know quite a few people in the auto industry. In fact I've probably put most of their kids through school — I've had that many cars. Occasionally in the course of a deal, you meet someone who becomes far more than a business associate. Gavin Williams, salesman extraordinaire and fellow petrol head, sold me a car some eight years ago and he and his lovely wife, Wendy, and baby Holly still spend some time over Christmas with us most years. They will always be special to me.

One day I took a call from the general manager of Scuderia Veloce Motors, Sean Lygo. He was calling to find out if I still had my Ferrari. I was very glad I could say yes at the time because it was my ticket to a day of unparalleled fun. I was off to a Ferrari drivers' day at Eastern Creek Raceway. Yahoo! I arrived at the track at about 10 a.m. in my 328, a beautiful, if impractical car. I parked alongside a Testarossa, which was parked next to a 348. This was paradise, I thought, as I headed for Pit Row. Around 30 people arrived, most in Ferraris, some in Porsches. We lined up the Ferraris for a photo opportunity just as a helicopter landed on the track in front of us. Mobile phones were abuzz as Gerhard Berger and Jean Alesi stepped from the chopper, and the event managers announced that they were going to take each of us for a spin in a new 348 Ferrari. They held a draw to see who was to ride with whom and I drew Jean Alesi — this had to be heaven. For anyone who doesn't know, these two drivers were at that time the F1 Ferrari drivers and they were in the country to compete in the Australian Grand Prix. I climbed in next to Jean and, firmly buckled in, we exchanged customary pleasantries and off we went.

Man, you have got to be joking . . . we were flying along at 180 kph before you could sneeze. This was incredible. Jean turned to me to ask, in his outrageous French accent, 'So, how do you like playing the Phantom?' What could I say . . . there he was, relaxed and comfortable, even getting chatty, lounging back with only one hand on the steering wheel while I was pinned, speechless, to the seat. I actually had my video camera on my lap but the G-forces were so strong that I couldn't lift it. The first lap whizzed by in a blink and the pits were merely a blur. Halfway round the second

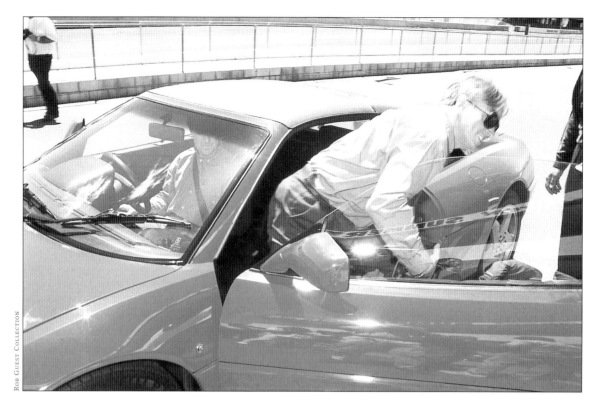

Getting out of a Ferrari 348 after two laps with Jean Alesi — note the smile.

lap, we both spotted a hare hopping onto the track. With an incredibly deft flick of the wheel Jean whipped the car's tail first right, then left and straightened out again, all at over 200 kph.

He was a lovely man and one hell of a driver. I have to admit (though I would not have thought it possible) to watching Formula One racing with even more interest since meeting Jean Alesi and taking that ride. What a ride! I know I wore a grin for a week. Gerhard Berger was more interested in driving Sydney car dealer Laurie Sutton's F50. In the end, I don't know whether he took any passengers for a lap, certainly not in the F50. Many concerned faces peered from the pits as Berger took the million-dollar monster screaming down the straight with clouds of smoke billowing from its rear. I heard that it was just burning in as it was so new. The sales pitch even worked, to a point. I was tempted to buy a beautiful jet-black 348. Isn't that what they wanted us to feel? Eventually I did sell my Ferrari, though not to buy a new one because I eventually grew weary of comments such as, 'Didn't I tell you to leave MY car at home?' I had a series of red cars for a while, including a Jaguar XJS Convertible and a 560 SL Mercedes convertible — all red . . . well, they go faster! Then I had a run on black cars.

I managed to scare myself one night, driving home after *The Phantom*. I was in the Sydney Tunnel in the Ferrari, with the roof off and the windows down. There was not a car in sight and I had the radio playing quietly, so I could just enjoy the beautiful roar of that pedigree beast as it permeated the evening air. I was exiting the tunnel when suddenly I heard a voice, which sounded, for all the world, like it came from someone sitting right beside me. They said, 'You are in the Sydney Harbour Tunnel and the speed limit is 80 kilometres per hour. Please reduce your speed!' Well, I almost drove into the tunnel wall! They had tapped into my FM band on the radio somehow.

These days they use a speed camera. Oh well, I don't want a Ferrari any more!

The Ferrari was very, very cool, but the fastest car I have ever owned was a jet-black Lotus Esprit Turbo. Zero to 100 kph in 4.2 seconds. Talk about snap your head back. Once again, totally impractical, especially on a hill-start where, in order to apply the handbrake, it is almost necessary to rest your forehead on the windscreen. I'm not exaggerating. This car was to be auctioned, brand-new, at Pickles Auctions in Sydney, and Gavin called to tell me about it. It had been a lottery prize that someone didn't want to keep. I went with Gavin in the daytime to check it out. We weren't allowed to test-drive it as the battery was flat and it was still covered all over with paint-protecting goo, applied at the factory. I did some checking and found that, new, it was worth about $215,000 plus on-road costs. I told Gavin that I had a show to do and couldn't be at the auction that evening. As he was planning to be there to buy some other vehicles, he agreed to bid on my behalf. That night the show began as usual, and at the first opportunity, in fact as the auction scene had just begun, I called Gav on his mobile. It turned out that the Pickles auction was also just under way, but as there were quite a few vehicles to be sold before they would get to the one we were interested in, we agreed to speak again at interval.

We completed the 'First Lair' (the boat scene) and I dashed back to my dressing room. 'No calls,' said Norman, who was intrigued by the fact that I was trying to do two things at once. At interval, as arranged, I called Gav again and he answered the phone with 'Next but one', so I hung up and anxiously left him to it. Ten, excruciating minutes later the call came. 'Rob, you own it!'

'Oh no,' I thought, as I realised in the same moment that I would have to sell my 500 SL Mercedes — I loved that car! Oh well. I took delivery about a week later. What a great-looking car the Lotus was . . . and fast! I was a happy lad, having paid only $130,000 for it. Cheap at half the price — did I say ONLY $130,000??? Anyone in their right mind would have thought that they couldn't lose with odds like those, a $100,000 discount. Yeah, right! Two short months later, Lotus brought out a new model, a special Anniversary edition, for just $165,000 — ouch! No sooner had this hit the market, than they released the V8 — double ouch. I finally sold this fine auto 18 months later, for $115,000. Well, it might have been worse — I could have been one of those poor souls who'd paid over $200,000. Imagine how they must have felt.

I've enjoyed some magical travel thanks to the music industry, and as I've said before, my career is forever twisting and turning, often in mid-air, changing direction on a phone call or a telegram or a fax. On one memorable occasion, Qantas had booked me to perform in one of three promotional concerts arranged for travel agents from around the Pacific. They flew me to Hong Kong with Jude and Tony McGill (my musical director for the show, who is also part of the wonderful trio Combo Fiasco) to perform on the Saturday night, the middle night of the series. Ansett had contracted John Farnham and band for the Friday night, and local entertainers performed on the Sunday night. Ansett arranged a cocktail party with John and the band and Qantas treated the delegates to a sumptuous banquet — in a very glamorous setting, complete with black velvet drapes, roses and candelabras (with real candles). Everyone was wined and dined in absolute luxury. I must say Qantas, especially Mr Groves, has class.

It was during this Hong Kong trip that I received a fax asking me to be at the Channel 7 studios on the day of my return, as they wanted to talk with me about 'Missing Pieces'. Curious and ever interested in a new challenge, I faxed back immediately, agreeing to be there. As promised, as soon as we were home I visited Channel 7 and they took me through the show. It was fascinating and I knew immediately that I'd thoroughly enjoy presenting it. The show involved putting people back in touch with each other, people from all over the world. The public were asked to answer questions that had remained unanswered, often for decades. I was in my element. We went live to air as phone lines buzzed and things moved at an unpredictable pace. Everything worked well but, as I have mentioned before, network budgeting executives often have bigger fish to fry and we were brought to an untimely close. A real shame, but that's showbiz.

One afternoon, at about the time of 'Missing Pieces', John Robertson called. Cameron had asked if I would be willing to perform alongside 21 other Valjeans from around the world at the 10th Anniversary concert of *Les Miserables* at the Royal Albert Hall in London. I readily agreed. I knew that to represent my fellow *Les Miserables* cast members at such a joyous occasion would be an incredible honour and an opportunity not to be missed. I took leave of absence for a few days and flew to London. I landed in the UK on Friday morning and immediately went sightseeing. You see, I have this theory that when you fly to London from Sydney, if you eat and stay awake until Bangkok, then sleep for the eight hours or so until London, you can arrive refreshed and ready to make the most of your time. Well, it worked for me. On the Saturday I had a rehearsal and afterwards Craig Schulman, the Broadway Valjean, and I went in search of an authentic, old-style English pub. We didn't have to look far, but funnily enough we wound up about 2 km from where we were rehearsing in an almost empty bar. Empty that is, except for Valjeans. There we were representing Australia and the United States, with the Valjeans from Iceland, Japan and Germany. This felt like 'Monty Python does *Les Miserables*', and we both burst out laughing.

On the Sunday morning, Noel Davis (he was my agent at the time), Jude and I decided to go out for a spot of breakfast. We were after a real English breakfast. After turning up our noses at 10 different places (my fault, I'm afraid) we came upon a small restaurant with a few chairs outside, and on an empty table was a plate of cold bacon and eggs and a mug of coffee. We smiled and walked on. As I passed by, someone from the very last table spoke to me. I stopped abruptly and announced to my companions that we were to eat right there. 'Why?' chorused Jude and Noel, in perfect unison. 'Because,' I said, 'RICHARD HARRIS has just told me that this place serves the best breakfast in London!' It's true! It was Richard Harris. We went inside and ended up going back every day. It certainly was a good breakfast, and from that moment on the humble bacon and egg breakfast has been known to us as the 'Richard Harris'. He even signed my musical score for the concert. Philip Quast, the best Javert in the world in my opinion, was lined up to re-create the role at the anniversary concert that night and I couldn't wait. Colm Wilkinson was also getting ready to perform the role of Jean Valjean, and when I asked him how he felt he said, 'Terrified! I haven't performed this role for eight years and there are 20 people out there who believe they can do it better than me!' I replied, 'No, you're wrong — there are only 19!'

An amazing event it was and an opportunity to revisit *Les Miserables*. *The Phantom of the Opera*, in the meantime, was due to move to Brisbane. We were still sold out and we knew that the reason for the move was theatre availability — theatres are booked a long way in advance. To predict the length of a run for a show of the magnitude of *The Phantom* takes a very, very big crystal ball and a great deal of guts. It's quite a gamble and a job I would never volunteer for. The role of Christine was to change again. This time Danielle Everett was to take it. She had been in the chorus understudying not only the role of Christine, but that of Carlotta, the diva, as well — a large stretch for any singer. Once again, I had a talented new leading lady.

As the family were growing and settling into friendships and schools we had a difficult decision to make. Our choices were: take the children out of school and hawk them around the country (not a great option); for me not to tour, which meant leaving the show (also not a great option); or for me to bite the bullet and go on my own, which seemed the only logical choice. This was the first time I was to travel without the family and I remember the day clearly. I loaded the car, put the ski boat on the back and headed north to Brisbane for a six-month stay. I flew home to Sydney each week on my day off to spend time with my family.

I had negotiated to live at Sanctuary Cove, on the golf course, even though I knew that the drive to and from Brisbane would take around 50 minutes each way. I enjoyed being away from the hullabaloo and a drive after performing always allows me to unwind, so it suited me well. Before the move, my dear Norman had become ill. He had a nasty cough, which progressively worsened. When John Robertson called me to say Norman had developed pneumonia I flew to see him straight away, but Norman, typically, acted as though he had nothing more than an ingrown toenail. He didn't want me to worry and kept saying, 'I'll be back soon'. He did get well enough to leave the hospital, but working with the show would have been too strenuous for him. I didn't know it at this time, but Norman was never to return.

Somewhat ironically at this time, *Les Miserables* came back to visit me. My original dresser for the show, before the wonderful Norman came along, was Chris Lyon. Chris is a friend and a heck of an assistant, but his presence was both a blessing and a poignant reminder of Norman.

Changes always seem to come in waves — my make-up assistant Sonia left the show at about the same time, to work on *Beauty and the Beast*. Andy Dowling had been head of the wig department so she was already an old buddy of mine when she took over from Sonia, making it an easy changeover. After a six-week break, cast and crew all arrived in Brisbane and launched straight into rehearsal. Once again we began, without costumes, fine-tuning the roles. David Caddick returned to oversee the music from the States, where he had just completed the movie *Evita* with Madonna and Antonio Banderas. Then Artie Masella arrived to oversee the direction as we tore the show apart and put it back together again. The place was abuzz, and *The Phantom* fever reigned once again.

Performers often describe the terrific feeling they get from being involved in a hit show. I have to say that being privileged enough to play the lead in a hit is exhilarating, to say the least. The reviews were fantastic from the day we opened and bookings were phenomenal. We were to play the next six months to sell-out houses and the name on people's lips all over the city was *The Phantom of the Opera*. I had the Lotus transported to Brisbane with a view to selling it there. Whether it was a wise decision I'll never know, but I eventually transported it all the way back to Sydney, and sold it later.

One Sunday, not long after opening the show, the phone rang. Norman had passed away. I recall having to walk away to find some space for myself at that moment. As we all find with the loss of a loved one, it was almost impossible for me to accept the fact that I would never see Norman again. We'd never share time or even joke again. Even so, the worst part was having to tell Chris and Amy that their 'Uncle' Norman had died. He was such a good man with a generous spirit and a heart of gold. I know that he is smiling now as I write this and he's watching over me as he did when he was alive. Even now, when I'm alone sitting in my dressing room, applying make-up, I find myself compelled, every now and then to look over my shoulder. I subconsciously expect to see Norman standing there, ready perhaps with one of those jokes or some constructive criticism. He was such a large part of my life and I miss him.

The following day I was to learn that Brian Stacey, my first musical director for *The Phantom*, the man who originally taught me the role, had tragically been killed in a motorcycle accident. The world was a brighter, better place because of this gentleman. We like to think he lives on through his beautiful music, but this is a sadder place with him gone. This was a dark time indeed for all of us who knew Norman and Brian.

Some of the guys had been hounding me to take the boat through to Brisbane for some skiing. Finally, in need of a little light relief, I agreed. I planned an early start, so I crept out to the car and hitched it to the boat trailer. Just as I began preparing the boat, my well-meaning neighbour came over. 'Nice boat,' he offered. 'What is it?' I told him a few details and he said, 'Bet she moves!' (No, I thought to myself, I bought it just to slow down my car!) Instead, summoning all the politeness I could at that hour, I simply said, 'Like a rocket.'

'Expensive?' he went on.

'Yep,' I said calmly, 'very' — wishing he would just leave me to it.

Then he said, 'Let me help you,' and just as I was trying to say, 'Please don't, I'm used to it,' he took over and coupled the trailer for me. So before I knew it I was driving away, waving goodbye to a complete stranger and beginning to feel a little ashamed at my lack of appreciation. After all, he had really only wanted to be helpful.

I waved to the security guard as I left the Sanctuary Cove compound, just so they could see it was me and not someone trying to steal my boat and car and I headed toward the freeway. I was chastising myself for thinking such horrible things about my neighbour. I really was upset with myself, but I managed to sidestep the guilt with thoughts of the great day's skiing ahead. I had decided to settle in for the 70 km drive and slowed to cross the only speed bump on the way to Brisbane. I was halfway over the bump when BANG, the trailer coupling came crashing to the ground. That dear neighbour for whom I'd felt such guilt had linked but not locked the connection. The trailer's arm, no longer attached to the towbar, rammed into the back of the car and with a sickening screech it came to rest on the road. It was saved from careering down the embankment at the roadside by the safety chain. I was now blocking one side of the road and the dolly wheel couldn't be used to raise the trailer back onto the towbar because it was firmly jammed under the towing arm. The boat and trailer weigh over 2000 kg, so I was absolutely, helplessly stuck! As the traffic started to build up behind me a semi-trailer pulled over on the other side of the highway. Two huge truckies were crying with laughter. They finally pulled themselves together and hopped out. One of them called out, 'Having a spot of bother, mate?' I offered no smart alec comment in reply this time. They blocked the other lane with their truck as they crossed the median strip. Then they grabbed the trailer's arm, and as though it were as light as a child's toy, they threw the coupling back onto the towball.

'There you go, mate,' they said, and I thanked them most sincerely as they ambled back to the truck. I checked the damage and there was a huge dent in the tarmac and an even bigger one in the car. Nevertheless, I was back on the road and the traffic could finally clear. As far as I'm concerned, never trust a Greek bearing gifts, and never let your neighbour within cooee of your boat!

Christmas came, at long last, and the family arrived to take over Sanctuary Cove. We had one of those battery-run golf buggies to drive around the shopping centre, in and because I had become a long-term resident, we were offered the use of the pool and other facilities at the Hyatt. We decided to have our family Christmas there and I invited my old friend Noel Davis to join us. As I've mentioned before, he used to be my agent and he was there in Brisbane as *The Phantom* company manager. A terrific guy.

What a hoot it turned out to be. The food was glorious and Jude and the kids decided to entertain the Hyatt guests with everything from 'Jingle Bells' to the 'Macarena' (with all the proper moves, courtesy of Amy). We finally left, well past dinner-time, carrying balloons and longing for a nap; it had been a long Christmas Day. I invited Noel to stay over, but he said he had to get back to Brisbane, so thinking he knew what he was doing, we waved him goodbye. The next day I found out that he had only driven about 10 km down the road before becoming too sleepy to drive. Apparently he pulled over for a kip, and as it was so hot he had taken off his trousers and dangled his legs out through the open car window. Remember folks, this was Queensland, it was summer, the road he was on was beside a river and it was night-time. Had he never heard of mosquitoes? Well, he certainly had by the morning — he had been bitten to within an inch of his life. What — me . . . laugh?! Sorry Noelie, I just had to mention it. Oh happy days.

People have asked me time and time again for my perspective on playing the role of the Phantom. They ask what it's like seeing the audience, experiencing the show, through my eyes. Well, I have often thought that having a miniature camera attached to me somewhere would be a real eye-opener for the audience. When you, the audience, see the Phantom and Christine enter the First Lair on the boat, you are transported to another place and time. Only those two people exist, and you share the unfolding of their story. On the other hand, we the performers see boat operators using remote control units, props people getting the next scene prepared, and a musical director watching your every move and listening to every note and placing the orchestra and orchestrations around you so that we all move in tandem.

I have to think very carefully before telling you about my world as the Phantom, for fear of wrecking the illusion. I decided to share my view, as I believe the illusion only lives because of the people I have just mentioned and the dozens of others who go unseen from show to show. The follow-spot operator, who sits cramped, high above the stage and can't move for over an hour at a time; the fly crew who make the scene changes seamless; and the front of house staff, without whom you wouldn't be able to sit comfortably to watch the show in the first place. As I've said before, my part is the tip of the iceberg only, the last cog, if you will, in the wheel that makes a show. Everyone around me that supports what I do deserves as much if not more credit.

9.

This is Your Life

ONCE AGAIN, SIX MONTHS had flown by and it was time to move the show. This time, to Adelaide. The turnaround was much quicker, but I knew this was going to be a busy time, as I had also arranged with Murray Thom to work with me on a second theatre album. We planned to release the album to coincide with the *The Phantom* opening in Auckland. Album planning is always a time-consuming exercise — what songs to put on, what to leave off, where to record. A myriad of choices and decisions had to be made and this was made more difficult for us as Carl Doy, my musical director, was in New Zealand. The faxes flew fast and furious across the Tasman and the time for Adelaide grew ever closer. We had a narrow time-frame to work with as I had to do the show and we had to finish recording in time to get the CD pressed and ready for sale. The entourage arrived in South Australia and the crew set to work unloading the 18 semis loaded with everything from the chandelier to spare masks. This time the chandelier was given extra special protection as gossip had it that it nearly beat itself to pieces on the way from Sydney to Brisbane. But that's another story.

Back in the rehearsal room, we fixed a few little glitches that had crept in and added a few subtle nuances here and there. We held the sitzprobe in the foyer of the Adelaide Festival Centre (a sitzprobe is where we rehearse the music with the orchestra only). I love this time, as you really get to hear the orchestra in full voice and we get to sing without having to think about anything else. After the show opening, the party was held in the train station, which had been decked out wonderfully for the special occasion, and as usual a great time was had by all.

Then it was time to get stuck into the album. Carl had been recording the orchestra in New Zealand and he'd been sending backing tracks to me to check for final keys and arrangements, etc. It was difficult to do it this way, but we didn't have another option. When the tracks were done, Carl flew over with the album's engineer and hired an Adelaide studio, where I was to be locked away until the vocals were completed. This album didn't have the complications of the first one, thank goodness, as I was able to sing every day, with full voice, and still do the show at night. Not that the songs were any less challenging, everything just went more smoothly. In just over a week, Carl and album engineer Doug Jane were winging their way back across the Tasman with a new album under their arm, ready to be mixed and pressed. Meanwhile, Murray had been hard at work getting the artwork organised for the cover and the video footage for the television commercials. Happily, I was able to call him to say I had been given permission to use the photo of me holding the mask at the Princess Theatre, in Melbourne. It was a great shot and it prompted us to call the album *Unmasked*.

We sold out the Adelaide season of the show, and we started the daunting task of labelling everything ready for the trip across the pond to Auckland. I remember the huge road crate that travelled with me being packed so tightly I needed two people to sit on it just to get the lid closed. I toured with a television, video, toast-maker, coffee machine, numerous photographs (framed, of course), computer equipment etc., and I'm sure that somewhere in there was a kitchen sink.

This was my second chance to return to New Zealand playing the lead in a sensational show. It was just as exciting and I was as proud as I could possibly be of the quality of work we were about to present. Sometimes New Zealand has to wait a long time for these shows to open there, and on many occasions the shows falter before getting that far. We found that many Aucklanders had come to Australia to see *The Phantom*, but this did not stop them coming to see it again and again in their home town. By that time, those in the know had calculated that the average number of times *Phantom* fans saw the show was an amazing six.

Once again, the crew worked crazy hours and again the set was incredible. Even though it had been loaded onto trucks, then jumbo jets and again onto trucks, it was as though the set had been at the Aotea Centre all along. These people are remarkable. I was living on Auckland's North Shore, and loved the view overlooking Rangitoto Island. Auckland is a truly beautiful city.

According to schedule, *Unmasked* was released, and it was a wonderful surprise to receive a gold disc on its release. It made all the hard work so worthwhile — not so much because it was an award from the industry, but more because it was evidence that the public liked what we were doing. It confirmed that we were on the right track.

The Governor-General's aide-de-camp called my agent at this time to arrange a date for me to receive my OBE It was to be held at Government House in Auckland and I was, as I'm sure you might guess, very, very excited. The day arrived and they had arranged a special function in my honour. They had been awaiting my return to New Zealand to collect this truly amazing tribute and I did feel guilty that it had taken me so long to get there. We had a lovely afternoon tea in the picturesque grounds and I tried hard to soak up as much of the atmosphere as possible before I had to leave at 4 p.m. to be ready for the evening show. Nothing could stop the curtain going up on another *Phantom* performance.

Even though I was in New Zealand, I still went home to Sydney every week to see my family. We used to do the Sunday afternoon show and I would get an early night and catch a flight at around 6.30 a.m. Monday morning. Thanks to the time difference, despite the fact that it was a three-hour flight, I used to arrive in Sydney at 7.30 a.m., with a full day ahead. Not so convenient was the return trip, as I had to leave Sydney at around 9 a.m. Tuesday morning in order to arrive in Auckland by 3.30 p.m. local time. The airlines never let me down, they have always managed to get me to the show on time. During the run in Auckland I clocked up my 2000th performance as the Phantom and John Robertson put on a supper for the cast, in my honour. That really was a season for milestones — I had the joy of bringing *The Phantom of the Opera* home to New Zealand, collected an OBE and then this special night. I was presented with a gold medal on stage

Opposite page: With my long-time friend David Hartnell, in front of a *Phantom* poster, Auckland.

and received faxes from around the world. Cameron Mackintosh sent a note which read, 'Many congratulations, you are now the longest-serving "living" mask and therefore utterly certifiable.' I was both moved and amused and, when Cameron became 'Sir' Cameron, I sent a fax to him congratulating him and I added that we were both now 'Sir'tifiable!

It was during the Auckland season that I was asked if I would agree (somewhere further down the track) to take over the role of Jean Valjean in the 10th Anniversary tour of *Les Miserables* in Australia and New Zealand. I still had a return season of *The Phantom* to perform in Melbourne and Perth, so it seemed ages away — it wasn't! Towards the end of the Auckland season, John Robertson called (many of my most memorable theatrical experiences have begun with a call from John). He told me that I would be leaving for New York on the following Monday to work on Broadway with the creator of *The Phantom*, the legendary Hal Prince. He knew I'd been playing the Phantom for five and a half years, and with a small gap of only two days in his frantic schedule he wished to spend that time working with me. I was ecstatic! I flew to Los Angeles, then immediately to New York. I hadn't been to bed for what seemed like a year and I was to start work firstly with David Caddick at his apartment the day after I arrived. I went to my hotel and tried to sleep — I was in New York! My mind would not stop. I slept spasmodically and woke the next morning as the noises of New York heralded the new day. I saw David early in the afternoon and we sang through some of the score of *The Phantom*. My voice felt tired so we didn't push it. That night I went to see *Titanic*. I can't understand why anyone would write a musical about a sinking ship. I did enjoy the experience, but I spent the whole evening waiting for the disaster. It's not a good thing to wait for.

The following day my call for onstage on the set of *Phantom* Broadway was 11 a.m. Hal had organised for two Christines to work with me — one from Miami and one from New York. The first thing I noticed was that there was glow tape everywhere. I presumed it was there to show the Phantom his way around in the dark. It was on the floor, the organ seat, everywhere. We went through a couple of scenes in company with David and Artie and the resident director of the Broadway production. I kept a mental note of everything that was said, and once we were finished I ducked into the nearest coffee shop and put it all down on paper. To get a couple of hours with someone like Hal is like having a Formula One driver teaching you to drive.

That night I booked in to see *Jekyll & Hyde*. I was blown away and, suddenly, I wanted to play it. Sadly, it was not to be. It's such a pity this show won't be seen in Australia or New Zealand. It has all the drama and the music that we have come to expect from a great musical. On my last night I went to see *The Scarlet Pimpernel*, a new production that was still in preview stage. It turned out to be a little like a cross between *Les Miserables* and *The Phantom of the Opera*. A period piece of wonderful drama; I believe that many parts have since been rewritten and the show is even stronger for it.

The following day I went to the airport and boarded my plane for the long flight home. It had been a whirlwind trip, but inspiring and informative. Hal was so kind and giving and it was good to see that what I had been taught was true to his plan. It was also confirmation that the integrity of the show had been maintained and nurtured just as he had conceived it, all those years ago. I passed on a few changes, subtle though they were, to our creative team to implement. I, too, had lots of fun working in the changes that the trip to New York had brought to my role.

Before we knew it, it was time to take the show back to Australia, back to where it all began: the Princess Theatre, Melbourne. The first time around, you couldn't get a seat to *The Phantom* for love nor money, and this season was to be no different. The advance bookings were great and we again opened to packed houses. It was wonderful to be back at the 'Prinnie'. I love that theatre. It is intimate and timeless. Shows take on a special magic there; a quality that's unique. I think *The Phantom* was made for this venue.

Auckland, at this time, had been having the most frustrating time with their power supply. The popular story was that the company that had been contracted by the council, 27 years earlier, to lay cables to supply the CBD with electricity had guaranteed their cables for 30 years. Well, they didn't quite make it! The Auckland CBD was without power. I can't vouch for the accuracy of the explanation, but the CBD definitely remained without power for months.

I had changed agents during that Auckland season. I found Penny Williams, a wonderful lady in whom I willingly placed my faith and confidence after only one conversation. We seem to think along the same lines and so we struck up a business and personal friendship that will last a lifetime. She is my sounding board, as well as a most valued friend. When Penny called and said she'd been approached by the Auckland Business Association with a request for me to sing at the reopening of the Auckland CBD, naturally I said yes. It was to happen on a Monday, my day off, and so I flew home to Sydney on the Sunday night and said goodbye to them again on the Monday morning as I went off to meet my Auckland flight. Arriving in Auckland, I was met at the airport and whisked away to the hotel at Sky City, where the function was to be held. I checked in, went to my suite and began running through the event schedule. Apparently I was to sing one song, then speeches, presentations etc., then sing another couple of songs. No problem. Carl had been hired to play the piano for me, so that side of things was well in hand. I just wanted to have a quick run-through with him and, as we say, top and tail the songs.

At the scheduled time, I was escorted to the theatre to meet Carl for the run-through. As I was to be a surprise guest, I was taken the back way, away from prying eyes. Carl was all set to go and we ran our songs, did a sound-check and I was escorted back to my suite. As we sat there, having coffee, there came a knock on the door. I opened it and standing there was a housemaid struggling with a foldaway bed. She asked me where she should put it and I told her she must have the wrong room, as I did not need one. She apologised and departed, well, almost. I was sitting facing the door, which had an opaque glass panel in it, and every few minutes I could see the silhouette of the housemaid and the foldaway bed passing back and forth in the hall outside. My escort for the event said she would be back to collect me at 7 p.m., which gave me an hour to have a shower and get ready.

Bang on seven, she arrived and we headed back to the theatre. I stood in the wings with Carl, waiting for the intro. I suddenly thought that if Carl was going to enter the stage from the right, it would be a better balance if I entered from the left. This meant I had to cross behind the stage, but as I headed off on my way I was abruptly stopped; grabbed in fact, and someone said, 'No, no, no; the lighting has been set for your entrance from this side!' So I stayed put.

Carl entered, I was introduced and entered the stage (from the right!) to the overture of my 'West Side Story Medley', which begins with the song 'Tonight'. I was into the verse when out of the corner of my eye I saw a television camera, closely followed by Paul Holmes. Carl stopped playing, the lights changed. The curtain behind me rose and Paul uttered those immortal words, 'Rob Guest, this is your life!' Oh my God, I thought — or did I actually say it out loud? They got me! Panic isn't a strong enough word — for the next hour and a half I was at the mercy of a television show.

I have to take a moment to explain that everyone, and I mean everyone, was in on this deception.

Jude had been talking to Touchdown Productions for months, giving them information and answering questions, helping them to compile my dossier. Penny was in on it, of course, and so was the Cameron Mackintosh Organisation, which in retrospect I see gave me leave way too easily. When I left my house that morning, Jude and the kids waved goodbye, but as soon as my car was out of sight Jude said to the children, 'You're not going to school today. Go and get out of your uniforms, we're going to New Zealand!'

Their plane left one hour after mine, or at least that's the way it was planned. They were even booked on a different airline, but my plane was delayed and there were a few critical minutes there where we may all have met up at Auckland airport. This explained the speed with which they whisked me and my baggage through and cleared me away from the terminal. When I went down for the rehearsal with Carl, everyone, including Mum, Jude, Chris and Amy, were in a dressing room backstage. The code used when I was around, was 'Elvis is in the building', so everyone knew to be quiet. Such a feat of stealth and organisation!

Out there, on the stage, Paul Holmes began to bring out people I had not seen since school-days. They showed video-clips from television shows I had done, though I couldn't (or refused to) remember wearing half the clothes they showed me in, let alone singing the songs. My goodness, I wore some outrageous outfits in those days. Everything from red satin suits (made by Mark Williams), to flares bigger that those on a '57 Chevy. But yes, it was me . . . rock'n'roll has a lot to answer for.

I was reminded of moments I would rather forget and occasionally taken back to times and people who have changed my life. Performers had flown in from far and wide and I was very touched that they gave their time to be part of my special night. When it was all over and the cameras were turned off, I decided to thank family and friends for being there, in the best way I know how — Carl and I had rehearsed, so why not sing? 'Anthem' was on the stand and, after all, it was the song that really began it all. So, after a few words, we did it. I had no idea, until afterwards, that the cameras were turned back on and this whole segment went to air.

We had a party in my suite and very late indeed we tucked Chris and Amy into bed. Amy in the fold-up the housemaid had, finally, been able to deliver while I was out. Poor lady, what a struggle. I never believed that I would be the subject of 'This is Your Life'. I had joked with everyone that if it were ever mooted, they were to stop it dead as I would not stick around. Knowing this, the producers must have been stressed to the max! Oh yes, it was because of that evening that the publishers of this book approached me, so without the show, you may never have read this.

The next day I bade farewell to everyone and headed back to Melbourne to continue performing in *The Phantom of the Opera*. Looking at the last few pages, one could be forgiven for believing that I was never at the theatre but gallivanting around the world doing other shows. The truth of the matter is that I was away from the main show very infrequently. Most of the other things I've mentioned have taken place on my days off, or have been tied to promotions and therefore been part of the show's 'machine' and at the direction of management.

The Saint James Theatre in Wellington had been recently renovated, for millions of dollars, so when I was approached to perform there with Elaine Page I leapt at the chance. We were to play in this magnificent 'new' venue on two consecutive evenings, with the Wellington Philharmonic. I contracted Michael Harvey to be my musical director and, once again, hopped on a plane. Rehearsals were limited, due to the fact that two acts needed to rehearse with the orchestra, which had only limited time available. The first show was a gala, the second was the official opening night. The Governor-General and his wife were there, as was the Mayor of Wellington and many other dignitaries. The shows were amazing — between us, Elaine and I sang every major song from every major musical, and came together for a duet for the finale. After the second show there was a knock on my dressing room door and when I opened it there stood Olivia Newton-John and Sir Cliff Richard — WOW! We spent an hour or so together before joining the official reception. Everyone loved the show and Wellington had a wonderful new theatre. Actually, I can't wait for a chance to perform in a theatre show there. The renovation was superb and I'm sure it is great for the city.

Melbourne's return season of *The Phantom* drew to a close and Perth would be the last stop. We had a rather sad and strange task ahead — we had to move the 'monster' for the final time. This was to be the first time a major musical was to be staged at the Perth Entertainment Centre. For us there was certainly no option — nowhere else in Western Australia was large enough to accommodate the production. The Entertainment Centre holds around 8000 people, but through clever curtains and new seating it was reduced to a lyric theatre of 2300. Not exactly intimate, but we needed this size of audience to make the show viable. You couldn't move in Perth without seeing *The Phantom* billboards, as huge as houses, with my ugly mug staring down at you above the words, 'He Awaits Your Pleasure'.

I found a place to stay on the beach at Scarborough — a beautiful apartment overlooking the Indian Ocean. Naturally, I was very happy to be beside the sea and, because management had worked a deal for us with a car firm, transport was no problem. The day after we opened *The Phantom*, Cameron Mackintosh announced that *Les Miserables* was to return to Perth. They also announced the cast and the fact that I was, once again, to play Jean Valjean.

It was during the Perth run that I was asked to sing the Australian national anthem for the first time. I was to perform before the rugby match between the Wallabies and the Springboks at Subiaco Oval. Luckily I was able to say yes — I have often said that I will sing either the New Zealand or the Australian national anthems, but neither if the two countries are playing against each other.

The Perth season was a great success but the end was drawing to a close. Before we knew it we were preparing to close a large chapter in Australian theatrical history. *The Phantom* was to close for the last time, seven and a half years after it opened in Melbourne. I had been with them for six and a half of those brilliant years. On closing night I gave my 2289th performance.

After packing up and returning to Sydney, I had a small break before starting rehearsals for *Les Miserables* in Melbourne. I contacted Polygram Records in Auckland, and with Michael Harvey as producer, we started to put together a Christmas album. We wanted to record it in Sydney and release it before Christmas, just before the *Les Miserables* Auckland season. The only downside to a Christmas album is that you have a very narrow window of opportunity in which to sell it, then it's all over for 12 months. We planned and recorded the album in North Sydney and Mike managed to get the masters to New Zealand on schedule. Then we were off to Melbourne to begin rehearsals for *Les Miserables*, so we shot the cover photo and television commercial in a small studio there. We then handed the whole job over to the record company and I was able to focus on the rehearsal process without distraction.

Rehearsals were wonderful, as they generally are. Gary Young, who played the bishop in the original Australian *Les Miserables* was now the resident director. Matt Ryan flew from England to help ease me back, and Martin Koch, also from England, worked with me vocally. It was like coming home — how I love that character. I have often said that if a small part of Jean Valjean rubs off on me then I would be a better person for it.

Some of the blocking had changed but the original direction, from Gale Edwards, was still embedded in my memory. So too, was the musical direction of Peter Casey. Deliah Hannah, a fellow Kiwi, was to take over the role of Fantine. She was in the original cast, all those years ago. David Dixon, my old mate, was playing Marius and a guy who was to become another firm friend, Scott Irwin, was playing Enjolras.

In the break before taking over *Les Miserables* I was contracted to sing 'This is the Moment' from *Jekyll & Hyde,* along with the national anthem, at the Melbourne Cricket Ground — the AFL Grand Final! It was one of those times when Penny says, 'Would you like to?' and I can barely wait for her to finish her sentence to say, 'Yes!' Then she told me that the plan was for Muhammad Ali to be driven into the stadium in an open-topped car while I sang. The day before the final, everyone gathered for a dress rehearsal and sound-check, and even then the atmosphere was electric. Everyone was charged and the show looked great. Add the crowds, the television presence, the buzz of a Grand Final and it's almost impossible to put the atmosphere into words. Harder still, to adequately describe the sensation of standing in the middle of that hallowed ground before the game. The excitement in the crowd is palpable and the focal point of that energy in the middle of the field is overwhelming. So I sang, with all my heart 'This is the Moment', and before the national anthem, as I was standing centre-field, an F-16 flew in, just clearing the floodlight towers. Directly over our heads the jet then took a 90 degree turn, straight up and nearly drove us into the ground with the force from its engines. Ahh . . . the best ride at the carnival. I was standing next to Michael Cormick, who had just finished *Beauty and the Beast,* and it made me smile when I thought that if this plane had fallen to earth, the world might have been one Phantom and one Beast less.

After the show, but unfortunately before the game, Jude and I had to leave, as we were to perform in a concert in Canberra that night. The limousine was waiting with two police motorcycles to escort us as quickly as possible to the airport. They were planning to hold the plane until we got there. It was like a scene from a movie. We climbed into the limo and waited. The bikes were there, but no policemen showed up. I guessed they were busy watching the game, so we left without them. The limo driver went for broke and got us to the plane with five minutes to spare. We caught the plane, arrived in time to rehearse, performed the show and crashed in a heap for the night. What a huge day!

Following just over two weeks of rehearsals for *Les Miserables,* I stepped in to take over the role for the last three weeks of the Melbourne season. This was just before Christmas and the transfer of the show to Auckland. It was great to tread the boards again as Valjean and my face was enjoying a well-earned rest from all the make-up it had been smothered in for *The Phantom* for all those years. I even had a beard again for the role, so I had no need to shave and my hair was growing long — YES!

The company was very strong and we were in great shape as we all went home for Christmas, to reassemble in the New Year in New Zealand. We went back into rehearsals full of energy and started previewing. I sang the New Zealand national anthem at the Auckland Cup Carnival — a wonderful tribute. However, the final preview, which was to an invited audience, I slipped on the barricade in Act II and my left ankle went from under me. It was sprained, there was no doubt about it, I couldn't put my foot to the floor. Stage management had seen me through the infrared cameras and realised I was hurt, so once I'd finished the barricade scene, having dragged Marius through the trapdoor, they were ready with ice packs to rescue me. I don't remember much about finishing that scene. I must have gone onto auto-pilot because all I can recall is the pain. The tough part was still to come — with a badly sprained ankle, I still had to carry Marius through the 'sewer'. The very thought of it brings tears to my eyes even now. I did manage to get through the show, though — just!! Noel took me to the hospital (he was once again my company manager), where we remained until 1 a.m., having x-rays taken, as we thought it might have been broken. Somehow, word got out to the press and reporters started to ask questions of the emergency desk staff. Those folks were wonderful the way they staved off the enquiries. The only thing they were prepared to tell them was that I was undergoing tests. Even so, the next day's banner headline in the *New Zealand Herald* read 'Star of *Les Miserables* May Miss Opening Night!' What they didn't know was that I would have to be DEAD to miss opening night! Luckily, Troy Sussman, who joined the first production back in Melbourne, was also in this production. Well, his father is a miracle worker when it comes to strapping injuries such as mine. He came over to my hotel and immobilised my ankle and it worked like a charm. The next day, he kindly came back to strap it again, for the opening night. Without him, I don't know if I would have been able to perform. I managed, and I didn't have to miss any shows.

Once again I was on the flight every Monday from Auckland to Sydney and back again Tuesday. I was flying more than some air crews were. One week a member of airport security wouldn't let me leave for Australia if I didn't promise to be back for the Wednesday evening show. Apparently her mother had been waiting months to see the show and was finally booked to see it on that Wednesday. I promised — and they let me go.

My Christmas album, by this stage, had sold beautifully. We wound up calling it *The Magic of Christmas* and I'm happy to say it became gold album number three.

The Auckland season had flown by and the next stop was Perth. We were back in the Entertainment Centre, which had been noticeably improved since our last visit. They had spent considerable money on sound-proofing the roof as, when it rained, the sound used to be deafening — we were all grateful. David, Scott and I were staying at Scarborough, where I had stayed while doing *The Phantom*. Perth is a wonderful place for playing on the water, so the lads and I decided to buy ourselves some new toys. Off we went to the Sea Doo agent and by the end of the day I was the proud owner of a Speedster Jet Boat and the boys both owned the latest Sea Doo jet-skis. We bought the jet-skis under the agreement that, when the show closed in Perth, the salespeople would ship the craft to Brisbane for us. Nice fellas, they lived up to the bargain. We had a blast! We even made the crossing to Rottnest Island — me in the jet-boat with my two 'baby ducklings' playing in my wake.

Flying back from Perth to Sydney each week can only be accomplished if you take the Red-eye Special, which leaves at 11.50 p.m. and arrives in Sydney at 6.20 a.m. It is cruel, to say the least. After doing a show at 3 p.m., getting home, showering and getting back into town to catch the plane you're feeling a little jaded. By the time you've endured the flight and morning finally arrives, you are pretty well washed out. Then on Tuesday morning, guess what? You get to do it all again . . . Flying doesn't really bother me though, I see it as a mental thing. I don't do much for the duration of the flight, but read, or eat, or sleep, so why should I feel so tired? I tell myself that I should be fine, and it works . . . sometimes.

So, we closed Perth and off we went to Brisbane. Back I went to Sanctuary Cove. (I'm a creature of habit, you see.) This time though, the road between my apartment and Brisbane was like a go-kart track as the road-works were terrible. Still, I loved getting into the car and driving after work. It gave me time to think and come back to the real world. The jet-boat arrived, but I didn't use it in Brisbane and ended up towing it back to Sydney at the end of the season. The show, again, was a wonderful success and before we knew it, alas, I was about to bid farewell to Jean Valjean, again.

Penny called, with her usual impeccable timing, to say that she'd heard from Jon Nicholls about a project he'd mentioned to me 18 months earlier. He wanted to know if I was interested in talking to them about *Jolson*. Suzie Howie had instigated our first meeting, but I had been under contract until that time and was, therefore, unavailable. So Jon sent me a script and he and Rob Bettinson, the co-author and director of the original London production, flew out from England so we could have a meeting. We clicked!

He was great and knew exactly what he wanted — that's my kind of bloke. They flew back to London with the knowledge that they'd found their Australian 'Jolson' and I had a new show to think about. I continued to love *Les Miserables* for the remainder of the Brisbane season, but a bitter-sweet feeling crept over the company toward the end of the run. Here I was, saying goodbye to Jean Valjean again and although I knew in my heart that someday, somewhere, I would find him again, I knew that this was the end of an era, another of those most moving of theatrical experiences. For 11 years I had been with the Cameron Mackintosh Organisation, and when this show closed, we would all be moving on, as Cameron had closed down his operations in Australia. A sad time for our theatre industry, but a necessity, as it seems that the business is undergoing a massive change. That, I suppose, is life. The big shows will still come, but I think the seasons they play will be shorter.

Odd things continued to happen in the show — some downright creepy and some pure comedy. One night, during the barricade scene, when all the characters around us are supposed to be dead, Marius stirred, as scripted, and I came to and looked up at Marius just as an ambulance roared past outside the theatre with the loudest siren I've ever heard, howling its arrival. I would love to meet that ambulance driver, just to tell him what he did as 2000 people guffawed and we stifled our smirks. The timing could not have been more inappropriate. I would defy anyone to try and play the next scene with a straight face. When David Dixon, who was playing Marius, and I emerged from our 'crawl-space' under the barricade, we could barely stand we were so desperately trying to stifle our laughter. The count-down to closing night began, and before we knew it, it was upon us. I miss Valjean so much, but I guess I always will.

I knew that the script for *Jolson* was a powerful roller-coaster of a role. It was non-stop and I knew it was a huge task I had laid out in front of me. In no time at all I was back in Brisbane preparing to do the advance presentation for the show's group travel bookings, something that I was more than used to, except this time I was performing the songs before I had begun the rehearsal process. We began rehearsals at the Betty Pounder Studios and for three weeks I ate, breathed and spoke Jolson. Rob Bettinson was wonderful. My call each day was 10 a.m., as I had requested the hour from 9 until 10 to go over the previous day's work, before moving forward. The dialogue was going to take time to learn, but luckily I had learned most of the 23 songs I was to sing before rehearsals began. This was a major advantage as it freed some of my mind and energy for the very demanding staging and movement. By the end of the first week I hurt in places I did not know existed.

Rob continued to be magnificent — he had such a great understanding of the Jolson character that, as the character came to life, every day was more exciting than the last. At the end of the three weeks of rehearsals, I had the show 'in my kicker' as Rob would say. Jolson, I had discovered, was a very complex man, who was only happy performing and when he was in the spotlight. They call him the greatest entertainer who ever lived, so to portray him on stage was both a privilege and an honour.

It was time to head to Brisbane, there were previews to do and then we were to open on 2 December. When you have had such an intensive rehearsal period, there comes a time when you

Review of *Jolson* — *Sydney Morning Herald*, February 2000.

really crave an audience. That time had arrived! Unfortunately, we still had to endure 'tech' week before we could have our audience. This is, as I've mentioned, the chance for everything that moves, lights up, goes bump, or is simply expected to look good, to be put through its paces and fitted into the show. I actually love this time — it's a time for fine-tuning. I can find that spot on the stage where the light starts and ends, get my sight-lines sorted out and get to know the musicality of the show with the new orchestra, who turned out to be exceptional!

Opening night arrived, and jangling nerves abounded. Rob brought me a gift, which I hurriedly opened before the show. It was a review of *Jolson*, written as though by a critic. Obviously Rob had described the show from his perspective and it was an enormous gift of encouragement, approval and support. The audience went crazy at the close of the show — we had plied, moulded, manipulated, romanced, cajoled and confronted these people for over three hours and it had paid off.

The show proved to be just as demanding, if not more, than I had imagined. As I said, it just didn't stop, but the pace of the show also meant that the time screamed by and, after seeing in the year 2000 on the banks of the Brisbane River, suddenly we were planning the move to Sydney. Sydney seemed ready for us, but what were they expecting to see? Did they think that I was going to do a Jolson impression, complete with black face? I don't think anyone really had a clue and that just added to the fun.

Jolson is a play within a musical, and so it offered me the chance to show that I could act. I did not have to sing every word the way I did in *The Phantom of the Opera* or *Les Misérables*.

On opening night, Sydney took us to their hearts and we enjoyed a huge response. Once the fun and frivolity of the first night party had faded into the morning, though, we settled down to the thing we love most — eight shows a week.

People came from far and wide, buses arrived from as far away as Dubbo, Newcastle and Goulburn, bringing people who had grown up with the music of the great Al Jolson. Some of those folk knew the songs as well as, if not better, than I did, and every one of them had a favourite. Mine is 'Sonny Boy', and every night I would sing it thinking of my Dad. He used to put me on his knee when I was three or four and sing it to me. I miss him so much.

I would have loved to have been a fly on the wall in one of those buses as everyone relived the show over and over again. People described to me busloads of Jolson fans singing 'Mammy', 'Carolina' and 'Swanee' as their buses rocked and weaved their various ways home. My job, in a nutshell, is to be a storyteller and that is a great story to tell. Hopefully we managed to give everyone a great night at the theatre, one that stays with them in their memories for a long time.

Jolson's run in Sydney was limited by many hidden factors — theatre availability was a challenge, and as the Olympics were looming, people's focus was changing. So it was with much sadness that I bid farewell to 'Al', for a while anyway. The following weeks were taken up writing this book and performing corporate shows, including a quick trip to Hawaii, where, once again, it wasn't until about the fifth day that I finally started to relax.

One Thursday night I was with Chris at a yo-yo exhibition in Saint Ives, Sydney, when my mobile phone rang. It was Penny. Here we go again, I thought, and indeed her call changed my life again. John Waters, who was playing Captain von Trapp in *The Sound of Music* had taken ill. The show's producers wanted to know if I would consider taking over. Penny needed an answer immediately and when I said yes, she said, 'Well, you'd better get home and pack because you have a costume fitting tomorrow morning at 10 a.m. and then a flight to catch at 3 p.m. tomorrow afternoon.' I was blown away, but off I went. It turned out that I had four short days to learn and be on stage as the Captain because the show was opening on the following Thursday. This just goes to show how wonderful and unpredictable this business is — when you least expect it, expect it! The phone will ring and the distant voice on the other end can throw your world into a spin and launch you into a whole new reality. On the way to the airport my phone rang once more. I answered. It was the unmistakable voice of Robert Newton, who was playing Uncle Max in *The Sound of Music*. He had taken the time to call personally and let me know that I had his support and that of the company. It was such a wonderful, generous thing to do, and I will never forget it. It meant so much. We have since become firm friends . . . thanls Bert.

I wouldn't change what I do for anything. I am so lucky to have been given the chance and the freedom to do something that I love, and I realise that I am among a fortunate few who have had this opportunity. This industry has been good to me and I will continue to learn and grow with every new project and undertaking. It's always changing and it's always exciting. I thank every person I have ever had the privilege to perform with. Every dresser, every usher, every co-star, director and musical director, every crew member and musician I have worked with has taught me in some way and added to my appreciation of this industry. I thank you all for making the canvas on which I paint so stable.

This is not the end, but the beginning. So the next time you see a show advertised, do yourself a favour — book a seat and allow yourself to be transported into a world of wonder.